Robert Smith has brought to the writing of baseball history the rare combination of literacy and a knowledge of the game's past. That a gifted novelist should possess the first of these two qualifications is not surprising; more impressive is his allegiance to accuracy.

Tom Meany, Frank Graham and Arthur Mann are a few who have similarly combined smooth technique with a reverence for facts, but they have all been actively connected with the major league scene. Smith writes from the point of view of a fan and exhibits the best qualities of that breed—compassion, constant wonder and a sort of sweet nostalgia. But he can let the irony flow, and if the occasion warrants, he can be mordant.

Until now the careers of the men elected to the Hall of Fame have not been examined as carefully as one might think. Their obvious deeds have been recounted in various books, some better than others; but here I think is a shrewd peek at their personalities. There is proper awe, but the maple syrup has been eliminated.

This is a book that the reader will want to finish in one sitting and then return to, again and again, for refreshment.

LEE ALLEN, Historian
National Baseball Hall of Fame and Museum
Cooperstown, New York.

Boston-Philadelphia at Boston, 1872. Standing: 4th from left, Anson; 8th, Spalding; 9th, G. Wright; 11th, H. Wright. O'Rourke is at Spalding's feet.

# THE EARLY DAYS

REFRESHMENTS. SODA

IN THE BEGINNING, BASEBALL WAS CALLED THE "NEW YORK" GAME BECAUSE IT WAS PLAYED EXCLUSIVELY BY NEW YORK GENTLEMEN'S CLUBS. BUT IT WAS SOON IMITATED, AND AFTER THE CIVIL WAR SPREAD ACROSS THE NATION. A GENTLE GAME AT FIRST, BASEBALL BECAME ROWDY AND ROUGH WHEN SPECTATORS DEMANDED IT

**MORGAN G. BULKELEY** as a baseball player, was strictly a "muffin"—the name given in baseball's earliest days to a man who played the game ineptly and entirely for fun, as a golf "duffer" plays golf. His presence in Baseball's Hall of Fame is due entirely to his year of service as first president of the National League, through the season of 1876.

Before that, Bulkeley had been president of the Hartford Dark Blues of the old National Association, one of the best of the early professional teams. And all his life he had been a famous baseball "krank"—the Dutch term used in the last

Morgan G. Bulkeley

Alexander Joy Cartwright

century to mean "fan."

In Bulkeley's day, there were not more than a few score professional ballplayers in the whole country. Boston's team, with Harry Wright and A. G. Spalding, had the best of them and Bulkeley had some of the others in Hartford. His team was so little appreciated there, however, that after the Association folded up, the Dark Blues were playing their "home" games in Brooklyn.

When William Hulbert of Chicago joined with A. G. Spalding to create the National League, they forced the organization down the throats of the eastern clubs, who could either join or see their players hired away from them. To salve eastern pride, after the League had been formed, Hulbert and Spalding agreed to let Bulkeley serve as president. After one season, Hulbert himself took over and in some books is still listed as the "first" president of the National League.

# ALEXANDER JOY CARTWRIGHT the man
who invented the "New York" game of baseball, never earned any fame as a player. When he and his playmates on Murray Hill, in New York City, first worked out the diamond in a

"Father" Henry Chadwick

Arthur "Candy" Cummings

vacant lot, about 1845, there were organized teams that played town ball (a roughhouse form of rounders) while other young men, who did not play cricket, played cat-ball, which was the poor man's version of the great British game. (Cat was short for catapult—a stick used to propel the ball out of a ring while players tried to see how many bases they could touch before it was recovered. One-hole cat was cat-ball played with one "hole"—a spot for grounding the bat, like the crease in cricket.)

Cartwright thought town ball, which permitted the plug-

11

Old-Timers' Game at Fenway Park, Boston, 1908, with A. G.
Spalding seated, 6th from left, above. Below, 2nd from right,

sits inventor of catcher's mask, Fred Thayer of Harvard. Tyng of Harvard, who first wore mask, seated 6th from left below.

ging of the runner with the small hard ball, was too rowdy, while cat-ball was rather too childish. His game combined some of the features of each, with a few ideas of his own. When it was first played, the number on each side was never set—it might be 6 and it might be a dozen. The game was played until one side or another, in even innings, had scored 21 "aces" or runs. But when it was formalized by the New York Knickerbockers, Cartwright's club, there were nine men to a side. The baseline distance of 42 paces has remained almost the same until today, and most of Cartwright's other notions are retained. The 9-inning idea, however, was borrowed from the Philadelphia version of town ball.

Before Knickerbocker baseball had made even half a stride toward becoming the National Game, Cartwright was off to Hawaii, where he lived out his long life, and where he was teaching his game to natives and to haole children before many people in the States had ever heard about it.

**HENRY CHADWICK** before baseball awarded the title to Abner Doubleday, was known throughout the land as "Father of Baseball." The title seemed to have grown upon him by common consent and many an old-time ballplayer always referred to him as "Father" Chadwick.

He had not, of course, invented the game at all. But he nourished it when it was new, and he remained loyal to it all his life. He even played the organized game for a season (with the Washington Nationals) and in 1858 he wrote the first rule book. He invented a shorthand method of keeping score (a method that was soon outmoded) and for many a season he acted as senior authority of the game, interpreter of rules, adviser, consultant, critic—and reporter of the game. He wrote for some of the earliest sports periodicals in the nation, covering cricket and football as well as baseball. But baseball was always the game he felt closest to.

British-born, Chadwick never failed to emphasize the British origin of the game and he tried, vainly, to conserve in the game some of the British amateur tradition. He was not opposed to professionalism, however. Indeed he welcomed it as far preferable to the hypocrisy of pretending that ballplayers took no pay. He was a determined foe of corruption and of organized gambling in the game. In all the baseball "guides" and "handbooks" that he edited, he argued for clean living and honest sport. The model baseball player, he once wrote, "plays the game throughout, whether winning or losing, to the best of his ability, and retires from the field apparently content with the result, whatever it may be."

# WILLIAM ARTHUR CUMMINGS has been

named the inventor of the curve ball. But in his day, right after the Civil War, several of the great pitchers threw curves. All Arthur Cummings did was to find out what caused a ball to curve and set out to control it.

Like all full-time ballplayers of his day, "Candy" was an "amateur," even though he earned most of his living by playing ball. But, when baseball was new, it was deemed shameful for a man to play it for money, so the great amateur clubs (like so many of today's colleges) recruited their athletes by assuring them of undercover payment, or jobs without work.

Candy, born in Massachusetts, was throwing clamshells across the backyard of his new home in Brooklyn when the idea of curving a baseball came to him. He practiced with a nickel baseball until he found out what caused the ball to dip or break; and soon after that he joined a teen-age ball club (Arthur was 14) and became their star.

Candy Cummings finally turned openly professional. He pitched for the New York Mutuals (Bill Tweed's team), for Baltimore, for the "old" Philadelphia Athletics, with the Hartford Dark Blues and the Cincinnati Reds, where he ended his career. Eventually there were many pitchers who could outcurve and outthrow him. But he remained the most famous of them all.

# ALBERT GOODWILL SPALDING for all prac-

tical purposes, invented the National League and so is largely responsible for the health and longevity of the professional game. His name is still imprinted on the baseballs used by the National League—but that is because he founded the company that manufactures the balls.

Hurley, Sub.; G. Wright, S.S.; Allison, C.; McVey, R.F; Leonard, L.F.
Sweasy, 2d B.; Waterman, 3d B.; H. Wright, C.F.; Brainard, P.; Gould, 1st B.

RED STOCKING B. B. CLUB OF CINCINNATI.

Spalding (left) swings bat in 1908 Old-Timers' game. He chooses up sides (right) in old style by fitting fingers on bat. (Top) picture shows first pro team.

17

Al Spalding originally rose to fame as the kid pitcher of the Forest City nine, from Rockford, Illinois, the first team to win from the supposedly unbeatable Washington Nationals during the first great baseball tour in 1867. Al was just 16 years old then, a lanky, long-armed, but graceful young man with a fiery underhand pitch. He went on from there to Boston, where Harry Wright formed a professional team, after the Cincinnati Red Stockings had folded up. With the Boston Red Stockings, Spalding became a national figure. His first season he pitched 30 complete games, and won 20 of them. Next year, he won 36, and the next year after that, he won 41, then 52, then 56. He might have gone on getting better and better, but the National Association (which was the only professional league then) was suffering from lack of patronage, from the influence of gamblers, and from the inability of most batters in the league to hit Al Spalding's pitches.

Rather than let his job fold under him, Spalding interested a Chicago fan, William Hulbert, in starting a new league, where there would be strict control of gambling and enforcement of contracts. The National League was born in 1876, with Spalding managing the Chicago club. He celebrated the new league by pitching 61 complete games that year and winning 47. That was his last season as a pitcher. Next year he played first and second base and in 1879 he turned over the manager's job to Cap Anson.

Spalding was president of the Chicago club from 1890 to 1891 and led the club owners in the struggle against the Players' Brotherhood in 1890. At the end of the century he waged a valiant fight against "syndicate" baseball and won that too. Meanwhile his sporting goods firm prospered. He began to publish the official guides and record books for the major leagues and supplied most of the official equipment. He even wrote the first complete history of the National Game (or had it written under his name).

At nearly every major turn in baseball's history the name of Albert Spalding stood out: in the first national tour in 1867; in the first one-hit game ever pitched (June 27, 1871); in the first baseball trip to England, 1874; in the beginning of the first permanent league; in the adoption of the first "official" ball; even in the name of the first 200-game winner: A. G. Spalding himself.

# GEORGE WRIGHT

before there was any such thing as "organized" baseball, was playing the game for a living. Born in 1847, in Harlem, New York (now a part of New York City), just two years after the game was invented, George began to play the "New York" game of ball as a boy. He played ball first for the Gotham club in New York when he was 17 years old, put in a season with the Philadelphia Olympics in 1865, then came back to play for the Gothams and the Morrisania Unions.

When brother Harry, who had gone to Cincinnati as a cricket professional, decided in 1869 to create an openly professional baseball club there, George was one of the first men hired and the highest-priced man on the team ($1400).

George could play everywhere on a ball club and at one time

George Wright, age 25          Brother Harry, age 37

or another tried every position. He liked shortstop best, however, and for a long time he was the best in the country at that position. He played barehanded of course and used to bring cheers by his boldness in spearing hot line drives (the ball then was far livelier than the modern ball). He was one of the first shortstops to cover second base when the second baseman had been drawn off the bag, and he ranged right and left to back up other players as few of his contemporaries ever did.

He made 304 hits out of 483 times at bat with the Red Stockings in 1869, with 49 home runs. By the time he entered the National Association, however, the ball had been dead ened. Still, he hit well over .300 for four of his first five years in Boston.

When the National League was formed, George played with Boston, then managed the Providence club for a season, came back to Boston as shortstop in 1880 and finished his career in Providence in 1882. Meanwhile he had founded the Boston sporting goods firm of Wright and Ditson.

# WILLIAM HENRY WRIGHT is properly called the father of professional baseball, for he organized and captained (in those days the field manager was the captain) the first openly professional team in baseball's history: the Cincinnati Red Stockings. He also established the first professional team in Boston (called the Reds), after the Red Stockings had disbanded, and the brought his team into the first professional league, the National Association.

Born in England, Harry as a youth served as a cricket professional with St. George's Cricket Club, who played their games on the Elysian Fields at Hoboken, New Jersey, where the first baseball club, the Knickerbockers of New York, also played. Harry learned the game there and took his knowledge to Cincinnati. His Red Stockings became National Champions in 1869. Harry was an outfielder then, but, when his kid brother George was not playing shortstop, Harry could fill in there and he occasionally took a turn as pitcher. When the league was formed, and Harry was manager of Boston, he continued to play regularly and remained in the line-up for 4 seasons. He played 1 game a season for the next 4 years, just to keep his hand in. But it was as an organizer and a manager that Harry made his deepest mark on the game.

He offered his counsel free to people from all over the country who were interested in starting baseball teams, and no one can count the number of baseball diamonds that were laid out as he patiently suggested, the number of ball clubs that were organized in accordance with his detailed advice, or the number of down-and-out players who were indebted to his kindness.

William Henry (Harry) Wright in 1872 led the first pro team in Boston. His shoes were old-fashioned even then.

The Providence Club in 1884 where Radbourne, far left, earned name "Old Hoss" by accepting full burden when Sweeney, left, holding ball, walked out on team.

ONCE BASEBALL BECAME PROFESSIONAL, EQUIPMENT, SUCH AS THE GLOVE AND MASK, WERE INVENTED AND RULES WERE OFTEN RADICALLY CHANGED. THE OVER-HAND THROW SUPERSEDED THE UNDERHAND TOSS, THE BUNTED BALL REPLACED THE "FAIR-FOUL HIT," COMBINATION PLAYS WERE DEVISED. THE PITCHING DISTANCE WAS LENGTHENED — AND BASEBALL BECAME SIMILAR TO THE GAME KNOWN TODAY.

**ADRIAN CONSTANTINE ANSON** was called "Cap" (the manager of a team in the old days was always named the "captain"). When he first entered professional ball. with the Forest City team of Rockford, Illinois (where A. G. Spalding made his start earlier), he was known as "Baby" Anson, or "the Marshalltown Infant." He had been the first white child born in Marshalltown, Iowa, and he played his first baseball there on a team made up almost entirely of his father and brothers. Twenty-seven years later, when Anson ended his big-league career, he was known as "Pop," for he was one of the oldest men still active in the game.

Anson was a mighty hitter all his life. As a first baseman, he was noted chiefly for his ability to stretch his 6 foot frame an extra inch or so to snag a high throw that seemed impossible for him to reach. As a manager, he was notorious as a rough-tongued "coacher" and bullier of umpires, opponents, and even fans. But as a batsman, he struck terror to the hearts of pitchers even when he was deemed too old to play. His hits were usually booming drives, streaking on a dead-level course to the outfield. He hit the ball where it was pitched and his drives might land in any field.

Anson was supposed to have invented, or at least to have been one of the first to practice the hit-and-run play. He stood loosely in the box, never setting his feet until the pitch was coming, and then he might choke up or swing the full length of his bat. He was a proud man and religious about his physical condition. In a day when most ballplayers ate and drank as heartily as they could afford to, Big Anse ate no fried foods, drank no strong drink, did not smoke, and avoided potatoes and sweets.

As manager of the Chicago team, Cap Anson won a devoted following who stuck to him no matter what the fortunes of the team. At last he became Pop Anson to his players and to his fans, and when he had to leave Chicago at last, his team was long known as "the Orphans."

**DENNIS BROUTHERS** from 1881 through 1885, was the hero of every small boy in Buffalo, New York, where he played first base for the Buffalo team of the National

Cap Anson after he "jumped" to Chicago, 1876.

Big Dan Brouthers hit a long ball for Detroit.

League. (He also played outfield and third base once or twice and pitched a little too.) Big Dan was the mightiest batsman of that day, a man who believed in swinging the full length of his heavy warclub and who could belt even a wild pitch beyond the most distant outfielder.

In his five seasons at Buffalo he never once hit for an average of less than .318 and his long home runs and mighty doubles were the talk of the town for years. When he and three of his teammates (Rowe, White, and Richardson), making up Buffalo's "Big Four," were sold to Detroit for $8000 in 1885 the transaction was a thing to marvel at. In Detroit, he continued to hit well above .300, as he did for 14 consecutive seasons in big-league ball. His high mark of .419 in 1887 was topped only by the great Cap Anson of Chicago. His lifetime average in the majors was .348.

Big Dan—6 feet 2, and 200 pounds, with a mighty mustache to go with his outsize frame—started and finished his career playing bush-league ball in and around Poughkeepsie, New York. Beginning his major league career with Troy, in the National League, he played with Buffalo, Detroit, Boston, Brooklyn, Baltimore, Louisville, and Philadelphia—and even came back in 1904, when he was 46 years old, to play 2 games with John McGraw's New York Giants. In every city he left memories of mighty wallops.

# JESSE CAIL BURKETT one of the greatest batters

of all time, was a pitcher when he joined the New York Giants in 1890. He won 1 game and lost 12, but he batted for .309. From that time forth, except for a season in St. Louis 12 years later when he pitched 1 game and lost it, and played some at shortstop and third base, he was an outfielder, and a great one. Only two other hitters (Ty Cobb and Rogers Hornsby) attained a batting average of .400 or better as often as Burkett did. He did it three times: 1895, 1896, and 1899.

Burkett was a small man, only 5 feet 8 inches tall. But he was fast and strong, an excellent bunter, and, batting left-handed as he did, quick to get down to first base.

Most of his days were spent in organized baseball. He became a professional at the age of sixteen in Scranton, Pennsylvania, and after 15 years in the majors (with New York, Cleveland, St. Louis, and Boston) he bought the minor league ball club in Worcester, Massachusetts, managed it, and played on it for 7 years. After that, he managed other minor league teams, scouted for the New York Giants, coached baseball at Holy Cross College, and in 1933, when he was 63 years old, was manager of the Lowell team in the New England League.

Jesse "Crab" Burkett

John Gibson Clarkson

In his 16 years in the majors, Jesse Burkett only five times hit for less than .300. His best year was 1895, when he won the championship with an average of .423.

As a batting coach, Jesse Burkett had but one secret to impart to his charges: the indispensable quality in a batter was "that old confeedience." Jesse had it to spare.

## JOHN GIBSON CLARKSON was known all his life

(a tragically short one) as a moody and sensitive young man. It required the tenderest handling to keep him pitching. Yet when he was on the mound there were few of his day who could match him.

Clarkson broke into the National League in 1882 before he

had turned 21, becoming a pitcher for the Worcester team in his native state of Massachusetts. He won only 1 game out of 3 with this club and found himself next season with Saginaw of the Northwestern League. In his second season there he struck out 339 in 40 games. Before the year was out he was back in the National League, this time with Cap Anson's Chicago White Stockings. He completed the 1884 season there by winning 10 of the 14 games he pitched while striking out 96. Anson thought handsome John was the best pitcher he had ever seen, but soon discovered that if Clarkson was scolded he could not pitch at all while, if the manager remembered to praise him, John would go out and pitch 6 games in a row.

In 1885 Clarkson had his finest year with the White Stockings. He appeared in 70 games, won 53 of them and lost only 16. He struck out 318. In July of that year he shut out Providence 4 to 0, allowing not a single hit. In 1886 Clarkson won 36 games out of 53, and the next season he won 38 out of 58. Then he was sold to Boston for $10,000, the same price the great "King" Kelly had commanded from the same club a year before. Now Clarkson and Kelly became the $20,000 battery and John began to win games for Boston: 33 in 1888, 49 in 1889, 26 in 1890, 34 in 1891, and 24 in 1892. He was not a strong-arm pitcher but strictly a curve-ball man. He had such strength in his long fingers that he could spin a billiard ball so it would run a complete circle on a table.

Clarkson, who was used to pitching day after day (in 1889 he pitched 2 games in 1 day and later went to the mound 8 days in a row), began to fade in 1892. His arm was sore and discouragement took much of the starch out of him. Boston released him and Cleveland signed him. But John never regained his form. He appeared in 34 games for Cleveland in 1893 and won 16 while losing 18. Next year his record was 8 and 8. He found it difficult to finish a game these days and was given to moods of black despair. He had been posting more bases on balls than strike-outs for the past few seasons and it came to him at last that his career was over. He went home despondent. He was committed to a mental hospital before he died and never fully recovered his sanity.

**CHARLES ALBERT COMISKEY** made his great contribution to the game by playing his first-base position wide and deep, ranging into the outfield, or up toward second, to catch flies or gather ground balls. In an age when basemen were closely anchored to their bags, this play created a sensation.

With the St. Louis Browns, Comiskey four times won the "National Championship" and completely revolutionized infield play by teaching all his infielders to back each other up, to shift positions according to the tactical situation, even to

The "Old Roman," Comiskey                    Hugh Duffy

drop back into the "outfield" to smother hard-hit balls. He was the first too to bring the pitcher over to first on a ball hit to the first baseman.

Comiskey, who was named the "Noblest Roman" by a sports writer, eventually became the "Old Roman," for he stayed in baseball all his life. He helped organize the American League and took over the Chicago franchise—a property that eventually became worth millions. The park he built to house his great Chicago teams still boasts of its "Bards' Room," where Comiskey's cronies, who called themselves "the Woodland Bards," used to gather after games, or in between, to drink and sing and celebrate the joys of baseball.

**HUGH DUFFY** who still holds the highest batting average ever recorded in the major leagues since the modern pitching distance was adopted (.438 in 1894), got his major league start in Chicago but earned his greatest fame in Boston, where he was one of the Heavenly Twins of the Boston Beaneaters' outfield. (Tommy McCarthy was the other.) A stumpy little Irishman who could run like a rabbit, he belted the ball heavily wherever he played. In 16 active seasons in four different major leagues, he only four times fell below .300 at the plate.

Born in Rhode Island, he spent most of his career in New England and stayed in baseball all his life. He was only 17 when he turned professional, as a catcher with Hartford in the Eastern League. He was still a scout for the Boston Red Sox when he was 84. In between, he played for Springfield and Salem (Massachusetts) in the minor leagues, then signed with the Chicago National League club in 1888. When the Brotherhood strike came in 1890, Hugh Duffy, like most of the stars of the day, jumped to the Players' League, then moved to Boston in the American Association and stayed in Boston when the Association was merged with the National League in 1892.

Duffy had a batting style much like that employed by Mel Ott in a later era, except that Duffy hit right-handed. Duffy too would lift his forward foot when he began his swing. Although he was (according to Cap Anson, Duffy's first major league manager) too short and too light to be a major leaguer, he had a mighty pair of shoulders and the balls he hit would travel like rifle shots.

Hugh Duffy became a manager when his playing days were nearly done, taking charge of Milwaukee, the Philadelphia Nationals, Providence, the Chicago White Sox, Milwaukee again, the Portland (Maine) team, Toronto, and the Boston Red Sox in 1921 and 1922, with time between and afterward spent in scouting. Active with the Red Sox almost to the day of his death, he would never tell his age in his later years.

William (Buck) Ewing,
wore two gloves
while catching for
the N. Y. Giants
in the 1880's.
Note old
side-buckle belt.

DING FROM LEFT TO RIGHT, THE PLAYERS ARE (TOP ROW) HART, McFARLAND, DAVIS, PRESIDENT COMISKEY, ISBEL
LLIVAN AND WHITE (MIDDLE ROW) WALSH, SMITH, ROTH, HAHN, DUNDON, DONOHUE, O'NEILL, TANNEHILL AND ROH
(BOTTOM ROW) TOWNE, ALTROCK, OWEN, PATTERSON, DOUGHERTY, JONES AND FIENE.

COPYRIGHT 1906
F.ER.BURKE
AMERICAN LEAGUE CHAMPIONS

The champion Chicago
White Sox, owned by
Comiskey, beat
the Chicago Cubs
in the 1906
World Series.

**WILLIAM EWING** was one of the best-loved professional ballplayers, by both players and fans, who ever lived. Buck, a gentle, good-natured, remarkably fleet-footed man, was probably the first catcher to throw the ball to second from a crouch. "It wastes time to straighten up," he used to explain. But it was many years before other catchers learned the wisdom of this.

Buck played his first ball with a club called the Mohawk Browns. Like most other professionals, of whom there were only a few score in his earliest days, Buck played nearly every position. He entered organized ball with the Rochester club in the National Association, then joined the great Troy Haymakers.

When the Haymakers disbanded, Buck, with most of the others, went to New York. In his first year with the Giants, Buck led the National League with 10 home runs. In 1889, except for one pitching effort, he was a full-time catcher and led the league in putouts and assists in that position.

Buck became a manager when the Players' Brotherhood League was formed and he took all the New York fans with him.

Up to the day of his death, fans in New York still talked of the day he stole second and third, then called out (he enjoyed ribbing the opponents this way) that he was about to steal home. He stole that base too with a wild dash and a mighty slide that was reproduced in a lithograph as "Ewing's Famous Slide" and sold all over town.

**WILLIAM ROBERT HAMILTON** stole more bases (797) than any other player who ever played in the major leagues, and scored more runs in a single season (196) than any player before or since, not excepting Cobb, Wagner, or Ruth. He made most of his base-stealing records, it is true, in the days before the catcher caught right up under the bat and before pitchers had learned not to allow baserunners to get a head start on their pitch to the plate. But Billy was one of the fastest men who ever played ball.

Playing for Kansas City in the American Association (a major league then) in 1889, Billy stole 117 bases. (Cobb's

Billy Hamilton stole 797 bases in his major-league career.

top season mark was 96.) Billy's lifetime major league total of almost a thousand stolen bases is 45 ahead of Cobb's total. And Billy played only 14 years in the majors while Cobb played 24.

Billy Hamilton did his best playing for Philadelphia of the National League, where he teamed with Big Ed Delahanty and Big Sam Thompson in the outfield. In 1894, Billy hit .398 and stole 7 bases in a single game, tying a record made by George Gore in 1881 and never reached by anyone since.

A short, solid left-handed hitter (5 feet 6, and 165 pounds), Billy had, in his 14 years of active play in the majors, only 2 seasons (his first and his last) when he hit for less than .300. His lifetime average was .344.

# TIMOTHY J. KEEFE was so marvelous a pitcher for

the Giants that some fans nowadays think he was just a myth. But Tim was a very real and very mighty right-handed pitcher throughout the 1880's. Beginning in 1883, Tim Keefe, who hailed from Cambridge, Massachusetts, won 30 games or more every season for 7 seasons in a row. In 1883, pitching for the New York Metropolitans of the American Association (the original Mets), Tim won 41 games and lost 26. In 1886, pitching for the New York Giants (owned, like the Mets, by "Truthful Jeems" Mutrie), Tim won 42 games and lost but 20.

Tim's most famous feat however was his 19-game winning streak in 1888, beginning on June 23 and ending on August 10. This record stood unmatched until Rube Marquard, also of the Giants, duplicated the feat in 1912. Oddly enough, both men achieved their effectiveness through the development of a baffling change of pace—called a "slow ball" in Tim Keefe's day. Because Tim learned to throw his slow ball with the same motion he used on his fast pitch, he was able to bewilder the most famous batters of his day. Tim was fast too and his fiery speed gave extra value to his slow ball.

Tim was not a big man. He stood 5 feet 10 and weighed 185. But he was strong and durable. He pitched for amateur teams around Boston when he was in his teens, starting with the Franklin Juniors of Cambridge when he was 18 years old. When he was 19 he was pitching in Lewiston, Maine, for an amateur team called the Androscoggins, after Lewiston's river, and he pitched for several other New England amateur clubs before turning professional at the age of 23. Amateurs in Tim's day were not always strictly amateur, for there was usually an overpaid job, with no real work to it, attached to an assignment with any of the fast amateur teams of the day. Tim's professional career began with the Utica club of the National Association in 1879 and he played that same year with both New Bedford and Albany. He started the 1880 season with Albany but joined the Troy team in the National League before the season was over. He pitched his first National League game for Troy in August, 1880, beating Cincinnati 4 to 2. Tim finished his career at the age of 37 with the Phillies, for whom he won 21 games in 1892 and 10 in 1893.

# WILLIAM HENRY KEELER the man who is supposed to have invented the slogan "Hit 'em where they ain't," was a .300 or better hitter almost all his major league life. Wee Willie played with the New York Giants, Baltimore, and Brooklyn in the National League and with New York in the American League.

It was in Baltimore that he attained his greatest fame, and his highest batting average: .432 in 1897. That season he hit safely in 44 consecutive games. An infielder when he started in the majors, he moved to the outfield when he came to Baltimore (after 2 seasons in New York and Brooklyn) and stayed there the rest of his career. A tiny man (5 feet 4, and 140 pounds), Willie was never a slugger but he was a master of the bunt and the "Baltimore chop"—a stroke he and his teammates perfected to bounce hits over the heads of charging infielders who were looking for a bunt. He specialized in a choked-bat swing, placing the ball carefully where the fielders had left room.

Before the rules prevented it, Willie would often tire a pitcher out by bunting balls foul, thirty or forty in a row. To Keeler, a bunt was not a sacrifice but a means of getting on base. He never gave up a "needless" out but would rely on his tremendous speed and his careful placing of the ball to get him safely to first.

Willie stayed in organized ball for 20 years, finishing his career with Toronto in the Eastern League in 1911.

Tim Keefe, the legendary
New York Giant pitcher.

Willie Keeler of New York,
Baltimore, and Brooklyn.

Boston Beaneaters in 1889 included Dan Brouthers,
3rd from left, top, Radbourne, sitting 2nd from left,
John Clarkson, next, and Mike Kelly, beside manager.

Mike Kelly, (left) was Boston's "$10,000 beauty"
when bought from Chicago in 1887. He prompted the
chant: "Slide, Kelly, on your belly! Slide, Kelly, slide!"

**MICHAEL JOSEPH KELLY** is a name that has lived in the language for more than a lifetime, in the catch phrase "Slide, Kelly, slide!" For Mike Kelly of Chicago and Boston was the greatest slider of his day—the inventor, it is said, of the hook slide. He was a great improviser on the field and took advantage of every loophole in the rules. Kelly was the first right fielder to move in close behind the baseline. He thought up the trick of dropping his mask on the plate, when he was catching, to discourage the runner from coming in too fast. He was (so he said) the first catcher to use finger signals to tell his pitcher what to throw and the first man to see the sense of passing these signals on to infield and outfield.

In Chicago, the fleet-footed Kelly, a strapping young man with a big black mustache, came into his own. Playing pitcher, catcher, every infield position, and the outfield, Kelly earned a devoted following.

He was sold to Boston in 1887 for $10,000 and was called, for a time, "the ten-thousand-dollar beauty." In Boston his popularity was as great as ever. He became manager there for a time, then his skill began to fade and he was sent to New York, returned to Boston, and allowed to drift into the minors.

More famous for his improvisations and for his daring base-running than for his batting or fielding, Kelly still managed to post a batting average of .315 for his years in the majors. His high mark was .394 in 1887, his first year with Boston. The year before, while with Chicago, he led the National League with an average of .388.

## THOMAS FRANCIS MICHAEL McCARTHY a
little Irishman from South Boston, was a menace on the basepaths, and he and his Beaneater teammates were always scheming new ways to gain an advantage over the opponents or find a loophole in the rules. Tommy was one of the first players to learn to steal the catcher's signals, when he stood on second base, and relay them to the batter. And he was adept at the hit-and-run—still a new tactic in baseball in his day.

Studio slide by Tommy McCarthy of Boston.

Tommy, according to veteran umpire Bill Klem, was responsible for a change in the rule governing the man on base after a sacrifice fly. The rule used to state that the runner could not leave his base until the fielder held the ball in his hand. So Tommy used to keep a caught ball bounding from one hand to the other as he ran in to the infield — and of course it was then too late for the runner to try to score.

In 1888, Tommy jumped to the American Association and began to play steadily in St. Louis. That year he stole 109 bases. He tried a spot of pitching but earned no decision, and even, in 1890, served as manager for a time. In St. Louis, he was "Little Mack" or "the Kid," but he was a big man at the plate in 1890, when he batted .351 and led the league in runs scored.

Tommy finished his playing days in Brooklyn, went to scouting for Cincinnati after that, and later coached baseball at Dartmouth, Holy Cross, and Boston College.

# CHARLES ARTHUR NICHOLS despite his slight stature (5 feet 9, and 135 pounds when he came to Boston in 1890), and despite the fact that the men who made the

selections for the Hall of Fame did not notice him for many years, was still the greatest pitcher who ever worked for the Boston National League club. Indeed some of his records have never been matched in either league. For 7 seasons out of 8, with the Boston Beaneaters, the Kid won 30 games or more. In his lifetime in the National League, where he pitched for 15 years, for Boston, for St. Louis, and for Philadelphia, Nichols worked in 582 games and won 360 of them. (In only 20 did he fail to earn listing as the "pitcher of record.")

The Kid never objected to pitching frequently. Once he pitched 3 days in a row, in different cities (in 1892) and completed and won all 3 games.

But in the Kid's day, pitchers did not loll on the bench or snooze in the bullpen when they were not scheduled to pitch. On his "days off" Kid Nichols often had to stand at the entrance gate and keep an eye on the ticket taker, then count the tickets afterward. One day at the Polo Grounds in New York, he counted 30,000 tickets. "That was tougher than pitching nine innings," he said.

Kid Nichols had no tricky deliveries as so many of his contemporaries had. He relied on speed, control, and change

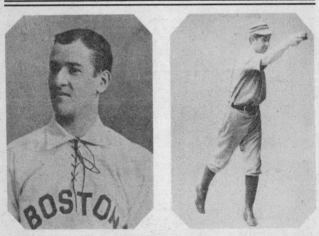

Kid Nichols won 361.

Copyright 1887.
Goodwin & Co.

— J. O'Rourke C. - Boston.~

OLD JUDGE CIGARETTES Goodwin & Co., New York.

Orator Jim O'Rourke poses in a Boston studio with ball on a string.

of pace. He never even had a curve to brag about. Yet he averaged about 120 strikeouts a season for 15 years in the majors.

**JAMES HENRY O'ROURKE** became known as "the Orator" early in his career, because he was a well-read man who loved to talk and who could lecture his teammates, or even his employer, for hours at a time about his legal rights. Jim started playing ball with the Bridgeport Unions in Connecticut when he was 15 years old, long before he was able to grow the luxuriant mustache that later became his trade-mark. He played his last professional game when he was 63. During the intervening years he played every position on a baseball team, and sometimes played them all on the same day. He also organized and managed teams, served as president, secretary, and treasurer of the Connecticut State League, and for a time acted as groundskeeper for the team he managed. (They played their games on the O'Rourke farm in Connecticut.)

Orator Jim took part in the first National League game ever played (Boston vs. Philadelphia, April 22, 1876) and he got the first hit ever made in the league—a long single to left, where Jim almost always hit them. Jim was catcher, first baseman, and third baseman with the Boston Red Stockings before the National League was born, and after that he became an outfielder. He was not the best of fielders (he once made 5 errors in one game) but he was a powerful pull hitter who terrorized third basemen with his slashing daisycutters. Jim O'Rourke deserted the Boston team when they tried to make him pay for his own uniform and his success in jumping to Providence prompted the creation of the "reserve rule" that has been a part of baseball contracts ever since.

Jim won his widest fame as a catcher and outfielder for the New York Giants in the 80's and 90's. In 1904, when he was 52, he talked his old friend John McGraw into letting him catch one more game for the Giants, and that was his last appearance in the big leagues. He got a hit that day too.

# CHARLES G. RADBOURNE became the "Old Hoss"

in a day when iron-man pitchers were commonplace. But Radbourne was the workhorse of them all. In his day, a pitcher did not leave the game when he grew unsteady: he went out to right field and played out the nine innings, for substitution was not allowed except in case of a disabling injury. But it did not weaken the team to have the Old Hoss in right field, for he was a solid hitter too and played there often when it was not his turn to pitch. Indeed, when he first took to playing baseball with the Peoria Reds (after quitting his job as railroad brakeman) he was known as a hitter and played right field regularly.

Rad's greatest year was 1884, when he won the pennant

for Providence almost singlehanded. When the other pitcher on the staff (Providence had only two regulars and one "change" pitcher) quit in a rage, Radbourne offered to shoulder the whole burden. He pitched and won 18 games in a row, lost 1, and then took 8 more, to salt away the pennant. That year he established the all-time record of 60 wins in one season. He pitched a no-hit game against Cleveland in 1883, when he won 49 games. In his 12 seasons in the major leagues (including 1 season in the Players' League) he nine times won more than 20 games.

**RODERICK JOHN WALLACE** a pale, angular young man with long arms and legs, was one of the original Cleveland Spiders, the tough, long-legged, and spider-armed crew that used to scare baserunners in the National League throughout the 1890's.

But Bobby was something more than a roughneck. Starting as a pitcher in Clarion, Pennsylvania, in 1893, when he was 18 years old, he moved up quickly to Cleveland, where he was converted to a third baseman, after two mediocre seasons on the mound (or "on the points," as they said in those days). He immediately began to pound the ball hard and he remained an infielder all the rest of his career, which lasted 25 years in the big leagues. After 5 seasons in Cleveland, he moved to the St. Louis National League team and played in that city 20 years, first in the National League, then in the American League, then back to the National League again.

In 1911, he became manager of the St. Louis Browns and played less frequently. He was a defensive player mostly, and deemed the best fielder of his time. After managing for 2 seasons, he turned over the job to George Stovall, but remained on the roster as a handyman, ready to play any infield position. In 1917, he switched back to the National League to put in two seasons with the St. Louis Cardinals as shortstop, third baseman, and second baseman. He played his final big-league game in 1918, when he was 44 years old. In 1937, he came back for a year to manage the Cincinnati Reds.

Bobby was perhaps the best-paid player of his time and before he quit the game was reputed to be the wealthiest.

**JOHN MONTGOMERY WARD** was a Columbia Law School graduate, and after his pitching career was over he held a big-league job for 10 seasons with his bat and his brain.

When John Ward joined the Providence Club in the National League in 1878, he pitched 35 complete games for them and won 22 of them. In 1880, with the same club, he pitched a perfect game against Buffalo, winning 5 to 0 and not allowing a Buffalo man to reach first base.

Ward's best year with the bat came in 1887 after he had joined the New York Giants. He hit .371 that year, while playing shortstop, and scored 113 runs. Ward, as head of the Players' Brotherhood, led the Brotherhood Strike in 1890 and helped form the Players' League. When the strike was over, he rejoined the National League as manager of Brooklyn and led the club for 2 seasons finishing in sixth place the first year and in third place the second year. Ward then moved back to the New York Giants to finish his career, and during those years he played in only a few games himself, retiring after 1894. He returned to organized baseball in 1911 as president of the Boston Club in the National League and also served as attorney for the National League, arguing at a congressional hearing in favor of the reserve rule that had prompted the rebellion he himself had led.

Roderick (Bobby) Wallace
stayed in the majors 25 years.

The Providence team in 1879 had some of the finest players in the
league, including Captain George Wright, standing 4th from right, John
Montgomery Ward, 2nd from left, and Jim O'Rourke, reclining on right.

47

# THE NEW

WITH THE NEW CENTURY CAME A MAJOR LEAGUE WHICH RECRUITED PLAYERS FROM SANDLOTS AND MINORS. THERE CAME ALSO THE RULING UMPIRE WHO WON THE RESPECT OF THE FANS WHO APPROVED OF A TIGHT CONTROL. THE LEAGUE PROMPTED INTER-LEAGUE CHAMPIONSHIP PLAY, LATER KNOWN AS THE WORLD SERIES, WHICH HELPED MAKE BASEBALL A BOOMING BUSINESS.

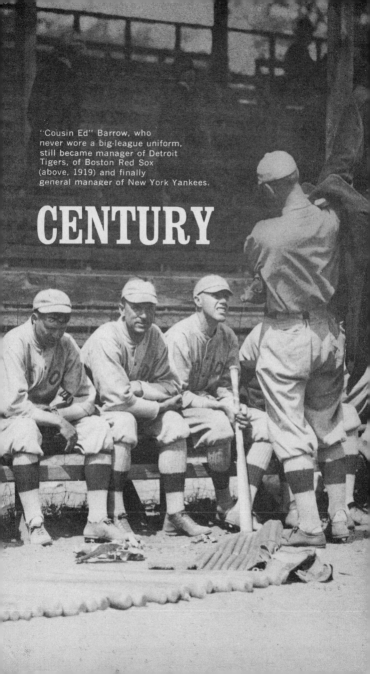

"Cousin Ed" Barrow, who never wore a big-league uniform, still became manager of Detroit Tigers, of Boston Red Sox (above, 1919) and finally general manager of New York Yankees.

# CENTURY

**EDWARD GRANT BARROW** a man who never liked night baseball and was opposed to the "farm system" of recruiting and training players, still did a great deal to modernize the game of baseball. He was the first baseball executive to call a halt to the practice of having ushers pry away from the fans the baseballs that happened to land in the stands. He was the first to put numbers on the players' uniforms, so the fans could identify them. He was the first to mark the outfield fences to indicate the distances from home plate, so fans could amuse themselves by contemplating the length of the home runs hit by the great sluggers under Ed Barrow's command.

Barrow owned the Paterson, New Jersey, franchise when the Atlantic League was formed and here he hired, and helped develop, a rookie named Honus Wagner, whom Barrow always considered the greatest baseball player of all time. Barrow became president of the Atlantic League and in this job got himself a reputation as a circus promoter. But the stunts he pulled, he said, were out of sheer desperation. He hired a girl pitcher, used heavyweight champion Jim Corbett as first baseman a few times, and had John L. Sullivan and Jim Jeffries for umpires.

When he got to the big leagues, however, Barrow eschewed all such hippodroming, for he felt baseball by itself was all the entertainment a man needed. In 1917, he became manager of the Boston Red Sox and joined his destiny there to that of Babe Ruth—the only man who ever called Barrow "Eddie." And Eddie Barrow was one of the few men who was able to discipline the Babe. It was Barrow who decided that Ruth should become an outfielder rather than a pitcher.

After Babe Ruth went to the Yankees, Ed Barrow followed, to become business manager and eventually president. While Barrow was there, buying players, making trades, and developing rookies, the Yankees won 14 pennants and 10 World Series, and put on display a long list of the greatest ball players ever brought into the same park.

**ROGER BRESNAHAN** started out as a pitcher with the old Washington team in the National League. He pitched

Ed Barrow when
he was president
of the Eastern
League in the
early 1900's.

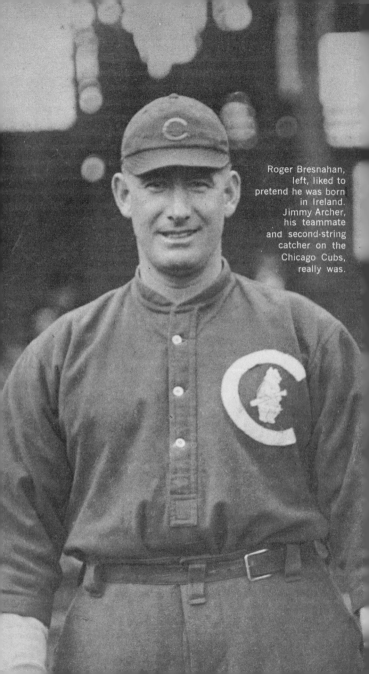

Roger Bresnahan, left, liked to pretend he was born in Ireland. Jimmy Archer, his teammate and second-string catcher on the Chicago Cubs, really was.

53

7 games in 1897, when he was 19 years old, and won 4 of them, but the team could not pay him the salary he wanted so he went back home to Toledo. By the time he got back to the big leagues, with Baltimore of the American League, he was both pitcher and catcher.

Bresnahan was unusually fast for a catcher and often batted first in the line-up. He was an unusually brainy player too — a schemer and a scrapper, just like John McGraw, who took Bresnahan along when he jumped from the Baltimore team to the New York Giants. In New York, Roger was a pitcher, catcher, third baseman, shortstop, outfielder, and assistant manager. He invented various stratagems for out-witting umpires and was given credit too for inventing shin-guards. But all Roger did was wear his shinguards openly, while other catchers were still ashamedly concealing them beneath their stockings.

Bresnahan played in only one World Series, the 1905 Series against Philadelphia, and he was one of the few men who hit hard in those games. He had an average of .313. In his best year with the Giants he hit .350 and stole 34 bases. He was skillful at working a pitcher for a walk and often tried hard to get himself nicked by a pitch to get a free ticket to first.

Bresnahan became a manager in St. Louis and nearly won a pennant in 1911 with the Cardinals. A train wreck in mid-season seemed to take the starch out of his team, however, and they fell back into the second division. After one more vain effort to come in first, Roger resigned as manager and went to Chicago, where he played 2 seasons with the Cubs, and served 1 season as manager. He came back finally to help John McGraw as coach and ended his active career as a coach with Detroit.

# MORDECAI PETER CENTENNIAL BROWN

was called "Three-Finger" Brown because he lost most of his right index finger, as a boy, when he was feeding field corn into a chopper. The loss of the gripping part of his finger gave him a natural "sinker" pitch that acted like a knuckle ball — dropping down sharply as it crossed the plate.

Brown played third base in sandlot ball and became an

able infielder. When he turned to pitching, he could still range all over the grass around his position to field ground balls. In 1908, with the Chicago Cubs, whom he pitched to a pennant that year, he accepted 108 fielding chances on the pitching mound and never made an error. (He also won 29 games that year.) In his 14 years as a major league pitcher, starting with St. Louis in the National League in 1903, Brown had only 4 losing seasons. In his great years with the Chicago Cubs, from 1904 to 1912, he had 8 winning seasons in a row, with 6 consecutive years in which he won 20 or more games.

Brown's pitch, a wide, fast-falling curve, caused most batters to top the ball badly and send it spinning out on the ground. With Brown on the mound, the Cub infield (Steinfeldt, Tinker, Evers, and Chance) became nearly impenetrable.

Brown could walk into a game without a warm-up in the late innings, get the batters out and go on to pitch nine innings in the next game. In 1908, between September 22 and the end of the World Series (which the Cubs won from Detroit) Brown pitched in 10 games within 22 days and won both ends of a double-header in that stretch.

# FRANK LEROY CHANCE like many big fellows of

his day, was known as "Husk"—he was 6 feet tall and his playing weight was 190. A solid hitter and a sure-handed fielder, Chance earned most of his fame as a manager. He led the Chicago Cubs for 7½ seasons and won 4 pennants and 2 World Championships with them. His 1906 team set a major league record of 116 victories.

Frank Chance started out as a catcher with the Cubs and played that position for 5 seasons, until his manager, Frank Selee, argued him into becoming a first baseman. He threatened to quit baseball rather than play first base in Chicago and it took a lot of words and a raise in salary to change his mind. But once the change had been made, he became a first-rate infielder; anchor man of the great double-play combination, Tinker to Evers to Chance. He succeeded Selee as manager in the middle of the 1905 season and after that the club, under his leadership, never finished lower than third.

When he was dropped by the Cubs in 1913 and signed with

Mordecai (Three-Finger)
Brown, (left) lost most of his
index finger in a corn-chopping
machine. This accident
gave him a "natural" sinker ball.

Frank Chance, peerless
leader of the Chicago Cubs,
did not want to be
a first baseman. But his
boss insisted and
Chance became a great one.

Happy Jack Chesbro
(above) won 41 games for
the New York
Americans in 1904.

The best infield in baseball
at the turn of the
century was this gang
from the Boston Beaneaters:
Tenney, 1b, standing;
Collins, 3b, on floor;
Lowe, 2b, left;
and Long, ss, right.

the New York American League club as manager, there was a parade and a gigantic floral tribute to welcome him to the Big Town.

Frank Chance's playing career was shortened by his inability or his unwillingness to get out of the way of inside pitches. He was hit on the head many times and long suffered from severe headaches. But he was tough and unyielding and in love with baseball and stayed in the game as long as there was anyone to make room for him. After he left the big leagues, he bought the Pacific Coast League Club in Los Angeles and managed it for the seasons of 1916 and 1917. In 1923, a year before his death, he came back to the big leagues to manage the Boston Red Sox.

## JOHN DWIGHT CHESBRO

**JOHN DWIGHT CHESBRO** the big tough lad from North Adams, Massachusetts, was nicknamed "Happy Jack" because he often wore a grin, and called "Algernon" (the current synonym for "sissy") for the same reason that a fat boy is called "Skinny." Jack was only 5 feet 9 inches tall but he was built like a small horse and he was hard as nails from his neck to his ankles.

Chesbro is the only pitcher who ever led both major leagues in won-lost percentages. In 1902, with the Pittsburgh team, he topped the National League with a record of .824. In 1904, with New York, he led the American League with a percentage of .759. That year he won 41 games for the New York team and came within one pitch of winning them a pennant. His wild pitch in the next to the last game of the season, against Boston, gave Boston the game and the championship. But without him, the New York team would never have been that close. Of his 41 victories, he won 14 in a row.

Happy Jack started playing professional ball at the age of 21, with Albany of the New York League, and moved that same season (1895) to the Springfield team of the Eastern League. He played with Roanoke and Richmond in the minors before signing in 1899 with Pittsburgh of the National League. He spent 11 seasons in the major leagues, winding up with the Boston Red Sox, in 1909.

Chesbro, whose specialty was the spitball, was one of the

last of the true iron men of the game, who were ready to pitch every day if they were asked. In 1904, in 55 games, he pitched a total of 454 innings. He struck out 239 that year and gave but 89 bases on balls. The crucial game that year, in which he made the wild pitch, he worked in because he insisted on it. He had been ordered to stay in New York when the team went to Boston to "win the pennant." He made the trip despite orders and talked Manager Clark Griffith into starting him in the first game there. Knocked out of the box in that game, he returned to New York with the team and started again 2 days later, his third start in a row. He was determined to win number 42 and to capture the pennant too.

Happy Jack actually got two of the six hits his team made that day, but, with two out and the winning run on third base in the ninth inning, one of his spitballs took off and sailed far over the catcher's head. Jack's friends always argued it was not a wild pitch at all. But others who saw it agreed the catcher could not have reached it with a ladder.

# FREDERICK CLIFFORD CLARKE was one of the greatest player-managers who ever performed. For 16 seasons he led the Pittsburgh team and for all but 4 of those seasons he was a regular in the outfield, batting over .300 in 8 of them.

He began his managerial career early, with Louisville in the National League, in 1897, when he was 24 years old; and that year, to celebrate his appointment, he hit for an average of .406, his best in the majors. He moved to Pittsburgh in 1900, along with Barney Dreyfuss, the Louisville owner, and most of the best players on the Louisville roster. Clarke stayed with Pittsburgh for the rest of his career. In 1925, he returned to Pittsburgh as a coach and the next year became a vice-president of the club.

Clarke, an Iowa farm boy, started playing baseball when he was selling newspapers in Des Moines and became a star in the Newsboys' League there. He began as a professional in the Nebraska State League, played half a season with St. Joseph in the fast Western Association and then moved to the Southern League, where he played with Montgomery and Savannah, before signing with Louisville, in the majors. He

Jack Chesbro (above) posing about 1909.
Jimmy Collins (right) in 1901 managed Boston A. L.
McGraw (right) greets Mgr. Fred Clarke of Pittsburgh (below).

Horner
Photo

made his major league debut on June 30, 1894, when he was not yet 22 years old. Before he ended his active career he had made 2703 hits in 2204 games. His lifetime average is .315.

As a manager of Pittsburgh, Clarke won 4 pennants and 1 World Championship and led his team in the first World Series ever played: the Boston-Pittsburgh Series in 1903.

## JAMES JOSEPH COLLINS

is well remembered today when a third baseman dashes toward the plate to make a barehanded scoop and throw of a bunt, for he made that play famous. He was not perhaps the first third baseman to handle a bunted ball this way, but he made a specialty of it and taught all those who followed him that it was the only way to beat the runner.

Jimmy, born in Buffalo, made his big-league start and made his reputation in Boston, where he played for both the National and American League teams.

Never a top slugger, Jimmy was still a timely hitter and in 1897, with the Boston Beaneaters, he posted a batting average of .346, his lifetime high. His lifetime average was .294. He was at his best, however, as an infield strategist. In his day, combination plays in the infield were not common and when he and Fred Tenney, Boston's first baseman, teamed up to nail unwary baserunners who wandered from the bag, the crowds used to scream in excitement.

Jimmy started playing professional ball in his home town, when he was 20. He played 2 seasons with Buffalo, then signed with the Beaneaters, who soon sent him on "loan" to Louisville. Next season he was back in Boston to stay for a dozen years. Under his leadership, the Boston Puritans of the American League won 2 pennants, in 1903 and 1904. They played (and won) only 1 World Series, however, for the New York Giants refused to play the representatives of the "bush league" in 1904.

## THOMAS HENRY CONNOLLY

British-born, never played baseball in his life. He started out as an umpire and finished his career as one. In the early 1890's, Tim Hurst, the National League umpire, who used to borrow a mask to umpire a game, discovered Tom Connolly umpiring for a Y.M.C.A. club in Natick, Massachusetts. He liked Tom's work so well he recommended him to the pros. Tom put in 4 seasons umpiring in the New England League, worked 2 seasons in the National League, and in 1901 joined the umpiring staff of the new American League. He stayed there 28 years, then in 1931 was made Umpire-in-Chief. Tom was a fair and fearless man who faced down the toughest of them, including John McGraw. In Tom's first year in the American League he thumbed ten players out of the game and made his order stick.

# EDWARD JAMES DELAHANTY of the five Delahanty brothers who played big-league baseball, was the oldest, the biggest, and the best. Big Ed was one of baseball's first great sluggers. Born in Cleveland, Ohio, just after the Civil War was over, he never saw the cork-centered ball, nor had a chance to hit when pitchers were forbidden to use foreign substances to roughen or darken the ball. But he struck some mighty blows just the same.

One day he broke a third baseman's ankle with a daisy-cutter that barely skimmed the dirt. Another time he laid into a well-worn ball so hard he broke it in two. And no other player in the major leagues has ever led both leagues in hitting: Big Ed led the National League in 1899; the American League, in 1902. Twice in his major league career he made 6 hits in 6 times at bat.

Playing second, first, and in the outfield, Ed began with the Mansfield team of the Ohio State league when he was 19 years old. Later, he joined the Philadelphia Nationals. He did not really begin to murder the ball, however, until 1892, when he was back in Philadelphia. That year he hit for an average of .312, and from that day forth he never dropped below .319. In 1899, he led the National League with an average of .408. He jumped to Washington in the American League in 1902 and immediately led that league with a mark of .376.

Bid Ed's greatest day came in Chicago in 1896 when he hit 4 home runs and a single in 5 times at bat.

Umpire Tom Connolly worked
in both National and American
Leagues over 34-year span.

John Evers (right) was the
brains of the Chicago Cub infield
for eleven seasons (1903-1913).

John Evers of Troy, N. Y. weighed
only 105 pounds when he
joined the Chicago Cubs in 1902.

Big Ed Delahanty, shown here in the 1880's, with Philadelphia, was still murdering the ball when the New Century
came in. Mustaches had disappeared from baseball by then.

**JOHN J. EVERS** when he joined the Chicago Cubs in 1902, weighed with a wet towel around his waist, 105 pounds, not really enough to qualify him for a job on a high-school team. The Cubs had taken him as a sort of makeweight in a trade, with a pitcher named Hardy. The price was $250 and the Cubs, after they took a look at the lantern-jawed youngster, thought they had been robbed. He was a grimly determined young man, however, and they gave him a try at shortstop, where he made 8 errors in his first 4 games. That would have finished him with the Cubs had not second baseman Bobby Lowe been injured. Evers was moved into that slot and stayed there. He'd have torn anyone apart who had tried to move him out.

Scrap, wit, determination, and speed kept John Evers in the big leagues. Like McGraw, Hughey Jennings, and Willie Keeler, he was forever scheming out ways to get an extra base or an extra run, or to seize any advantage over an opponent. He was no heavy hitter, yet he managed to get on base an inordinate number of times and twice actually hit over .300. With Joe Tinker and Frank Chance, he became the pivot man in the most famous infield combination in the game; and he was probably the ablest fielder who ever played second base, except for Eddie Collins.

Nicknamed "the Crab," because of the manner in which he scuttled about the infield, and the testy nature he displayed in his dealings with umpires and opponents, Johnnie Evers, after winning fame with the Chicago Cubs, went on to the Braves to become a hero in Boston. Here he teamed with another tough little character named Rabbit Maranville, to needle, cajole, scheme, encourage, and beseech his team-mates into a pennant—a miracle it was called and the credit was given to Manager Stallings. But Johnnie Evers, who was playing baseball in his mind through every waking hour, was the real spark plug.

**URBAN CLARENCE (RED) FABER,** one of the last four spitballers who were allowed to employ their specialty after this delivery had been outlawed, was also perhaps the only baseball player of Luxemburg ancestry. Born in Iowa in 1888, big Red spent his entire big-league career with one team—the Chicago White Sox.

Red was a tireless pitcher who toiled long and hard for a team that seldom finished in the first division. Yet he won more than 20 games in 4 seasons and in 1917, when his club did get into the World Series, he won three Series games. His best year came early in his career. In 1915, when he was 26 years old, he worked in 50 games for the White Sox and won 24 of them, while losing 13. He struck out 182 batters that year, the best he ever did in that department.

Red Faber was a switch-hitter, but he threw with his right hand. He stayed in the big leagues with the White Sox for 20 seasons and pitched over 4000 innings of baseball. A bad arm kept Red out of the 1919 World Series, in which several of his teammates were besmirched by charges of throwing games. But Red came back in the 1920's stronger than before, to win 21 games or more three years in a row. In 1922, with 21 victories, he posted his second-highest strike-out total: 148. Red was not a fireball pitcher nor a strike-out king. He relied heavily on his dipsy-doodling spitball to keep the batters rolling the ball to the infielders.

Faber actually did pitch for another major-league team, but his work was unofficial. Immediately after he had been purchased by the White Sox, Red was offered on loan to the New York Giants and went on a world tour with them. He beat his own club 4 times on the trip. Faber started his pitching career with St. Joseph's College in Dubuque, Iowa, and entered professional baseball with Dubuque in the Three-Eye League. While with Dubuque he pitched the first perfect game in minor-league history, beating Davenport 3 to 0 without letting a man reach first.

Red Faber, one
of the last
of the spitballers.

**CLARK CALVIN GRIFFITH** the Old Fox of major league baseball, was a very young fox when he started playing organized ball in Bloomington, Illinois. He was not yet 19 when he pitched 14 games for Bloomington and won 10 of them. He made his final active appearance 26 years later, as a pitcher for Washington in the American League. He stayed in organized baseball all his life, as manager and finally president of the Washington Senators.

As a major league manager, Clark Griffith never had a pennant winner, although his Senators won three pennants after he became president. His foxiness showed itself chiefly in his shrewd dealing in ballplayers. He combined veterans and youngsters to turn a last-place team into a pennant contender. When he started in Washington, Griffith seemed like a miracle man. He took over a ball club that had never placed higher than sixth and put them in second place 2 years in a row. Griffith was also a showman and more than once hired a ballplayer for his ability as a clown. Griffith was one of the original organizers of the American League and he put together the first New York team in that league, through wily "raiding" of the National League rosters. This skill at finding players (or managers) when he needed them earned him his nickname and remained his stock in trade.

Clark Griffith was pitching for the Cubs in 1900. In 1901 he jumped to the White Sox.

**HUGHEY AMBROSE JENNINGS** was one of the most famous graduates of the old Baltimore Orioles, in the days when they were the toughest team in the National League. Hughey was a little fellow, only 5 feet 8, but he was tough and full of fight. When he was playing shortstop for Baltimore he had a private motto: "Hit or get hit." If he could not get hold of a good pitch, he did not hesitate to get his body in the way of the ball, so he could get first base for free. His left side, in those days, was almost one wide bruise from the pitched balls that had hit him there.

Hughey's strategic skill and his burning desire to win earned him more fame than his bat did, but he did post 5 good over-.300 averages in 1894 and the seasons immediately following, when the pitching distance had been increased to 60 feet 6 inches. He was a one-man show on the coaching lines, especially when managing the Detroit Tigers, from 1907 to 1920. His battle cry of "Eeee-yah!" was famous all around the circuit and fans used to join him sometimes in this scream of triumph. He would wave both arms, with his fists tightly clenched, and kick one foot in the air when he emitted this cry, which eventually became his nickname.

When he began to slow down as a player he turned to managing, in the minor leagues first (when Baltimore had

Hughey Jennings in his famous pose, yelling "Eeee-yah!"

lost its major league franchise) and then in Detroit, where he earned even greater fame as a manager than he had known as a player.

A crafty batsman who, like all the Orioles, was a skillful bunter, Hughey had a lifetime major league batting average of .314. He 4 times led all National League shortstops in fielding percentage. In his 3 years as a major league manager (1907-9) he won 3 American League pennants for Detroit.

# BYRON BANCROFT JOHNSON is honored as the

man who founded the American League and became its first president. But Ban did far more than that. It was he who first insisted that the flagrant bullying of umpires must cease and that umpires hired by the league be backed up in their decisions even though an entire ball club, including the owner, should be arrayed against them.

Johnson never played professional baseball, but he was a college catcher. After graduation he became a reporter for the Cincinnati Commercial-Gazette and gave as much time to writing about baseball as his employers would allow. When Charles Comiskey left his job as manager of the Chicago National League team to manage the Reds in 1892, Johnson joined him and a few other in planning the Western Association — a minor league that hoped for major status — with teams in Detroit, Grand Rapids, Indianapolis, Kansas City, Milwaukee, Minneapolis, Toledo, and Sioux City. In 1899, by a mere change of name, this grouping became the American League.

Johnson was a strong president but not all his edicts won immediate acceptance. He tried for instance to put an end to "organized rooting" on the part of spectators, who had begun to form in groups to make loud noises in concert, like college boys at a football game. The fans, however, simply would not obey and eventually rhythmic clapping, cheering, booing, and even cries of "Take him out!" became a part of baseball tradition.

On the field, however, thanks to Ban Johnson, the baseball umpire now controls the game, for he knows that his orders cannot be countermanded by manager or club owner.

Bancroft Johnson, a former sports writer,
founded a new major league in 1901.

**WILLIAM J. KLEM** a tough little man who never
played big-league baseball, is perhaps the most famous
umpire who ever lived. Known as "the Old Arbitrator," Klem
almost by himself raised the standard of umpiring in the
National League. He was cool, determined, and convinced
that he was right. He permitted no baseball player to take
liberties with him and he devoted himself to his job with a
religious fervor. Indeed, just before his retirement, he an-
nounced at a dinner given in his honor: "Baseball is not a
game with me—it's a religion!"

Bill Klem, who wound up his career as supervisor of um-

Bill Klem, "the Old Arbitrator,"
would never admit he had called a
play wrong in his life.
No player dared disagree.

Umpires, in the old days,
required a megaphone man to
announce the batteries.
Bill Klem holds mask;
Connolly, next to megaphone.

pires in the National League, always maintained control of the baseball game he was umpiring. Players who approached him to argue a decision were warned: "Don't cross the Rio Grande!" The "Rio Grande" was a line drawn in the dirt by the toe of Bill Klem's shoe. If the player stepped across it, he was out of the game, and he knew it.

Bill Klem taught umpires to stay on top of the plays, so that their decisions could be made on the basis of a close view of what had happened. He invented the behind-the-plate stance that all umpires use today.

# CHRISTOPHER MATHEWSON when he first

played baseball for pay, was a cross-handed batter, strong, awkward, extremely willing, and only 14 years old.

His most famous pitch was named the "fadeaway" and it is compared to today's screwball—a reverse curve. But he also had a "dry spitter" that must have been a form of knuckle ball. He was a brainy pitcher, and a strong one who never seemed to tire. In 3 successive seasons with the New York Giants (1903-5) he won 30 games or more. And in the World Series of 1905, he won 3 games for the Giants— all shutouts. In 16 full seasons with the Giants he won 20 games or better 13 times. His high mark was 1908, when out of 56 games he pitched, he won 37 and lost 11, setting the "modern" record for wins in the National League. He also set the modern league record for strikeouts, with 267 in 1903. He pitched 2 no-hit games: one against St. Louis in 1901 and one against Chicago in 1905.

A master of control and an easy worker, Mathewson could go inning after inning without giving up a base on balls. Between June 19 and July 18, 1913, he pitched 68 innings in a row without allowing a walk—the record. In 1916, when his left arm (which was not his pitching arm) began to pain him, he went to Cincinnati to become manager there. He pitched only 1 game for Cincinnati and won that 10-8. He left this job to enter the army in World War I, was gassed in the trenches, and came back to act for a time as coach with the Giants. Soon afterward he was made president of the Boston Braves and held this position until his untimely death in 1925.

Gentle Christy Mathewson and tough John McGraw
(right), his manager, with the N. Y. Giants about 1903.

# CORNELIUS McGILLICUDDY

**CORNELIUS McGILLICUDDY** was known all his life as Connie Mack, for that was the way his neighbors in East Brookfield, Massachusetts, shortened his name so they could pronounce it. Connie, like most young males in East Brookfield, started to work in the local shoe factory. In his spare time he played baseball and soon played it well enough to make a living at it. He kept on making his living at the game, with his hard hands, his quick wit, and his shrewd brain, until he was 88 years old.

Called "Slats" as a boy, Connie early in his career teamed with another skinny lad, named Frank Gilmore, to become the Bones Battery — Mack catching and Gilmore pitching. Together they formed the best combination in the Connecticut State League. Connie was not the greatest catcher nor the heaviest batter of his day. But he owned the sharpest tongue and the quickest wit, and he talked many an able batter out of a base hit. In the National League, which he and Gilmore entered (with the Washington Statesmen) in 1886, Mack soon won fame as "the talking catcher," and fans used to gather just to enjoy the sound of his comically high-pitched voice.

Connie Mack first became a manager with Buffalo in the Players' League during the Brotherhood Strike but wound up with the Pittsburgh Nationals when the strike was over. A broken ankle received when he blocked the plate against Herman Long of Boston slowed Connie down, so he began to see the end of his playing career, and he was quick to accept an offer to manage the Pittsburgh team in 1894. He remained an active manager for another 55 years — with Milwaukee of the Western League and then with Philadelphia of the new American League, where he also became the owner of the club.

Connie Mack is best remembered now for the manner in which he used to run his team from the bench. Always dressed in hard collar, hard straw hat, and business suit, Connie waved his fielders into position with his folded score card — placing them, he once explained, with no false modesty, "so the fly balls would drop in their hands."

Connie won 9 pennants with his Philadelphia Athletics —

At left, Connie Mack, 90, and
Cy Young, 86, meet at Cooperstown,
N. Y. in 1952 to participate
in ceremonies at National
Baseball Hall of Fame.

Above, veteran Connie Mack,
50, talks with the
young president of the
Connecticut State League,
W. J. Tracey, in 1912.

In 1905, manager Connie Mack won his first American League pennant with this club. Chief Bender (whom Connie always called Albert) is at his right shoulder. Kneeling in front of Bender, Rube Waddell.

85

although in its earliest days his team was hard put to pay the groundskeeper—and his teams took 5 World Championships. Even when Connie was nearing 90, his team was sometimes in the thick of the race and Connie still found time to appraise young ballplayers and to write long letters, in a steady, legible hand, about how great some rookie catcher might be "in years to come."

Iron Man McGinnity firing "Old Sal," his underhand pitch.

## JOSEPH JEROME McGINNITY became famous as the Iron Man in 1903 when he pitched 5 double-headers for the New York Giants, winning 3 of them (in the same month) and dividing the other 2. He was a tireless pitcher. Using a half-sidearm, half-underhand pitch he called "Old Sal," he seldom struck a man out, but the pop-ups were numerous. Often he could retire the side on 5 or 6 pitched balls.

Joe was 28 years old when he finally landed in the big leagues, with Baltimore of the National League. He won 27 games his first year, then moved to Brooklyn (when Baltimore was dropped from the league) and won 27 more. In his first 6 days on the Brooklyn team he pitched and won 5 ball games but his fame did not spread across the nation until he began to win double-headers for the Giants.

He won only 9 games in his first year with New York, perhaps because he was busy playing second base and the outfield as well as pitching. But in 1903, he won 31 and in 1904, when the Giants won the pennant, Iron Man McGinnity won 35. In his 11 years in the majors he never had a losing season.

After he was through in the majors, Iron Man McGinnity earned his title all over again by pitching for 17 more seasons in the minor leagues, winning a total of 204 games there. In his final season, with Dubuque, a team he was managing, at the age of 54 Joe won 6 out of 12 games. He "retired" then to go back to the big leagues as a coach.

**JOHN JOSEPH McGRAW** is famed today because of his accomplishments as leader of the New York Giants, whom he managed for 31 years, and with whom he won 10 pennants and 3 Worlds Championships. But before he came to New York, he was known all through the baseball world as the tough little third baseman of the Baltimore Orioles, a scrappy, hard-hitting, quick-thinking and fast-moving little Irishman with a thin bony face and prominent ears, who feared no man and apparently felt all umpires were his mortal enemies. A forceful, even overbearing man, he had almost as many enemies as he had friends; but most of the men who played for him were fiercely loyal to him and some of them, becoming managers themselves, spread the McGraw gospel throughout baseball, imitating his pet plays, his training methods, his strategy, so that his impress on baseball was as great as that of any man who ever played the game.

As a player, McGraw shone brightest in Baltimore where he and Willie Keeler perfected the bunt and especially the foul bunt, which they used to wear pitchers down. But little John could hit the ball hard and in 1895 attained a batting average of .374. That year he stole 69 bases and in 1898 he stole 73. His lifetime batting average was .334. It was in Baltimore that McGraw learned the baseball strategy that was to make

John McGraw (left), near
the end of his career as
Giants' manager.

Wilbert Robinson (above),
led the Brooklyn Dodgers to a
pennant in 1920.

him one of the two or three great managers of all time. Some he learned from Ned Hanlon, his manager there, and the rest he learned from his teammates, as they sat up late nights to devise tricks, tactics, signals, and stunts to win the ball game next day. Winning was McGraw's religion when he was on the baseball diamond, and close teamwork, which meant loyalty and readiness to give all for the team, was the chief article of his faith.

Starting as a Sunday semi-pro at the age of 17, McGraw worked quickly up to organized baseball. He was a pitcher when he started but was soon switched to shortstop and finally to third base. He entered organized ball with Olean (New York) of the New York-Pennsylvania League, and went from there to Cedar Rapids, in the Illinois-Iowa League. In 1891, before the season was over, he quit Cedar Rapids to take a job with Baltimore in the American Association and landed in the National League when the League expanded to 12 clubs and added the Baltimore franchise.

He managed Baltimore in 1899, was sent to St. Louis next year to become manager there, and then jumped to the Baltimore team in the American League in 1901. A season and a half with Ban Johnson, who did not approve of abusing umpires, was enough for McGraw and he jumped back into the National League to take over the New York team and to turn it within a few seasons from a seventh-place club to a pennant winner.

When he retired in 1932, his fame was world-wide. Many baseball men who learned their strategy from him still mention his name with reverence.

# WILBERT ROBINSON spent so many years (1914-1931) as nonplaying manager of the Brooklyn Dodgers, who were often called the Robins in his honor, that many fans forgot that he had ever been a ballplayer himself. Yet he had 17 seasons in the majors, as a catcher with an occasional stint at first base. One season at Baltimore (1896) he batted .354. And on June 10, 1892, he made 7 hits (6 singles and a double) in 7 times at bat.

Robbie was one of the most aggressive and vocal members

of the scrappy Baltimore Orioles, who started in the American Association and wound up in the National League. To stay on that team, a ballplayer, besides being tough and aggressive, had to be smart and able to extemporize on the field of play. These skills helped make Robbie into a successful manager. But before he took over in Brooklyn, Robbie managed the Baltimore club in the American League, stayed with them when they landed in the Eastern (minor) League, and worked three seasons as coach with John McGraw and the New York Giants.

Robinson won only 2 pennants with the Brooklyn Dodgers (1916 and 1920). But his team was always in contention and was always unpredictable. There was always excitement at the Brooklyn ball park and the club prospered with Robbie at the helm.

Robbie's 1916 champions, like so many Brooklyn clubs, seemed to be made up of players nobody else wanted. But Robbie urged and schemed and maneuvered them into the flag, beating out the other 3 eastern clubs in the league by a close margin.

**JOSEPH BERT TINKER** head man in the Tinker-to-Evers-to-Chance double-play combination, spent all his major league career in Chicago.

Never a strong man at the plate, Joe topped .300 only when he was in Cincinnati. His great fame was earned by his fielding, and by his unerring teamwork in making the Cubs' infield impregnable through the early 1900's. Joe was not a tall man, only 5 feet 9, but he was solidly built and fleet of foot. In 1908, when the Cubs won the pennant, Joe topped all the shortstops in fielding percentage and in assists. In the World Series that year he handled 27 chances without an error.

He and Johnny Evers, the second baseman, played together like parts of a machine, using private and silent signals to indicate who was to cover second base on the coming play. In this way they were often able to smother hit-and-run plays by closing the expected "hole" in the infield. Yet for years

Denton True Young was called "Cy."
He said it was short for "Cyclone."

The start of a famous double play:
Tinker, to Evers, to Chance. Tinker
has just tossed ball to Evers, in
pivot. Evers drags his foot across
the base to make the first out and
prepares to throw over to Chance.

Rube Waddell liked to be called Eddie.

he and Evers did not speak to each other off the field.

Born in Kansas, Joe Tinker played his first professional baseball in Coffeyville, Kansas, joined the Denver club of the Western League when he was 19 years old, but finished that first season with the Great Falls-Helena team of the Montana State League. He advanced to Portland of the Pacific North-West League next season and led the league's shortstops in fielding percentage, in putouts and assists—and in errors too. He was promptly brought up to Chicago. He did not really come into his own there until Frank Chance was made manager. Then he and Evers and Chance took over the defensive strategy and made the Cubs nearly unbeatable for the next five years.

## GEORGE EDWARD WADDELL was "Eddie" to

his friends and would punch a stranger in the nose who called him "Rube" to his face. But finally he grew to like the name and applied it to himself when he urged fans in St. Louis (in signs he painted on the sidewalk) to "come out and see Rube fan 'em out!" That was toward the very end of his career, after he had earned national fame as a great pitcher and a great eccentric in Philadelphia and in several minor league cities.

In the big leagues, the only man with patience enough to handle Rube, who loved to take days off for fishing, or for riding fire engines, or for playing marbles with kids, was Connie Mack, for whom he did his best big-league pitching in Milwaukee and Philadelphia. Playing for Connie Mack with Milwaukee in the American League, Rube struck out an average of 5 men a game. When he settled down (more or less) in Philadelphia with Connie, he reveled in the new fame that was his and responded with some extraordinary pitching. In his first year, 1902, with Philadelphia he won 23 games and struck out 210, leading the league in that department as he was to lead it five more times.

In 1908, when Waddell would no longer respond to discipline, Connie had to trade his big Rube to St. Louis, where he came back to trim the Athletics with 16 strikeouts in one game—a record that stood for years. Although Rube won 19 games in each of his first 2 seasons in St. Louis, he never again attained the heights he reached with Philadelphia, where he won 27 games in 1905, while losing but 10.

# DENTON TRUE YOUNG called Cy (for Cyclone) was

the pitching marvel of all time, reliable, indestructible, and frequently unhittable. He pitched more games than any other pitcher in baseball (906), pitched for more years in the majors than anyone else (23), and won more games than any pitcher before or since (511). He also established a record for consecutive hitless innings (23). That mark was set in 1904, when Cy was 37 years old. That same year he pitched a "perfect" game (allowing not a single batter to reach base) for Boston against Philadelphia. He had previously pitched a no-hitter, in 1897, for Cleveland against Cincinnati in the National League; and in 1908, when he was 41, he threw another no-hitter for the Boston American League club against the New York Highlanders. In the minor leagues when he was pitching for Canton against McKeesport (Tri-State League) in 1890, he threw a no-hit game too and struck out 18 batters.

In 1890, he joined the Cleveland club of the National League. He pitched 8 full seasons for Cleveland, never winning fewer than 21 games and one season winning 36.

After 2 years in St. Louis (26-15, 19-18), he signed with Boston, in the new American League. He pitched there for 8 seasons, winning 33 games his very first year. In 1903, he won 2 games for Boston in the first World Series ever played between the National and American Leagues. In 1908, he was sold to Cleveland, and in 1911, at the age of 44, he jumped the league fence still another time, to sign with the Boston Braves. He won 4 games for them and lost 5 before calling it a career. His pitching arm was still strong enough, he insisted, but he could not field his position as fast as he used to and the opposition was wearing him down with bunts.

When Cy was 80 years old, actively farming in Newcomerstown, Ohio, he wrote to an inquirer concerning the speed of two fast-ball contemporaries, Amos Rusie and Walter Johnson. "Do not believe," he wrote, "that either one was quite up to me in speed."

ALTHOUGH THE SPEEDY CORK-CENTERED BALL WAS INTRODUCED IN 1911, THE GAME STRATEGY WAS STILL BASED ON THE DEAD BALL. DOMINATING THE ERA WERE THE PITCHERS WHO DISCOVERED HOW TO HOLD BASE-RUNNERS, WHICH CUT BASE-STEALING IN HALF. DESPITE THESE ADVANCEMENTS, STEALING, BUNTING AND SCHEMING REMAINED OF GREAT IMPORTANCE IN THE DEVELOPMENT OF THE GAME.

# DEAD BALL

John Franklin Baker became "Home Run" Baker in 1911 when he hit two home runs in the same World Series. But his real strong point was his sturdy and agile work with the glove. He was one of the best-fielding 3rd basemen in the game

DAYS

**JOHN FRANKLIN BAKER** actually hit fewer home runs in his major league career (93) than Babe Ruth hit in two successive years (114 in 1927-28). But Frank was hitting them when the ball was "dead" and home runs were a rarity. He led the American League in home runs 4 years in a row, with 9 in 1911, 10 in 1912, 12 in 1913, and 8 in 1914. But he got his nickname "Home Run" by winning 2 World Series games with home runs: in 1911 and in 1913. And in 1911 he hit 2 home runs in the same World Series.

Frank was a standout third baseman. As a hitter he had a lifetime major league mark of .308 and the highest average he achieved was .347 in 1912. As a fielder he led his league in putouts in 7 seasons and in 1917 and 1918, when he was with the New York Americans, he led all American League third basemen in fielding percentage. In 1914, in 4 successive games, Frank accepted 25 chances at third base without an error, making 10 putouts and 15 assists.

A powerful right-handed farm boy who batted left-handed, Frank was the left-hand corner of Connie Mack's $100,000 infield — supposed to be the best fielding crew ever put together. With Stuffy McInnis, Eddie Collins, and Jack Barry, Frank Baker formed a Maginot Line against enemy hitters, ranging far out on the grass or in front of the infield position to handle more chances than any rival third baseman in the league.

**CHARLES ALBERT BENDER** like all Indians in baseball, was known as "Chief." His own chief, Connie Mack of the Philadelphia Athletics, always addressed him as Albert, however, and this seemed more fitting for this quiet, easy-going young man who was one-quarter Chippewa Indian. (His father was Dutch and his mother half-Chippewa.)

Chief Bender learned his baseball at the Carlisle Indian School in Carlisle, Pennsylvania, and he entered professional baseball with the Athletics the year after he graduated from Carlisle.

Bender was only 19 when he joined the Athletics. He was a poised young man all the same and he stepped into stardom without a flutter. In his first season, 1903, Chief Bender won 17 of the 34 games he worked in. Four of his first 5 seasons were winning seasons and his eighth season with Connie Mack was his best. That was 1910, when he won 23 games and led the league in won-lost percentage.

Bender, who had the steadiest nerves in the game, also had remarkable eyesight — as sharp as that of the greatest hitters.

Chief Bender pitched in 5 World Series for Connie Mack, worked in 10 games and won 6 of them. He led the American League in won-lost percentage three times while he was with the Athletics: in 1910, 1911, and 1914. He played most of his remaining years in the minors.

# MAX GEORGE CAREY who started out in life

named Maximilian Carnarius, was never a great slugger; but he holds an impressive collection of major league records, most of them because of his speed. He was fast on the bases and fast getting on base. He was swift in the outfield and swift crossing the plate. Carey holds the modern National League lifetime record for total stolen bases: 738. He led his league in stolen bases ten times between 1913 and 1925. In 1916 he stole 63 bases.

Max was adept at reading a pitcher's movements so as to get a quick start. He was not a wild man on the bases like Cobb and a few others, but once he took off for the next base, he usually made it. In 1922, he attempted 53 steals and was successful 51 times.

In the outfield, Carey accepted more chances than any other National League outfielder before him: 6702. Six times he made more than 400 putouts in a season in the outfield; and he established a league record by playing more games in the outfield than anyone else: 2421. In 9 seasons he led all National League outfielders in putouts.

Born in Terre Haute, Indiana, Carey set out to study for the ministry at Concordia College, in St. Louis. But they had a baseball team there and young Max became a pitcher, playing shortstop in between whiles. With his studies completed, Carey joined the South Bend team, and was placed in left field. When he moved up to Pittsburgh (after stealing 86 bases

Chief Bender pitched in
five World Series,
won six Series games.

Home Run Baker (left),
favored old style
of turned-up collar.

Max Carey, Pittsburgh
speedster, studied for
the ministry.

in 96 games) young Carey still worked out at short from time to time. But the outfield was where he stayed—and it was the outfield rather than the ministry that proved to be his calling.

Max was a switch hitter, although he was a natural right-hander. He batted lead-off for Pittsburgh and one season (1922) scored 120 runs. In 1925, he made his top mark as a batter: .343.

# TYRUS RAYMOND COBB like Babe Ruth, deserves a Hall of Fame all by himself, he stands so far ahead of all his contemporaries in nearly every department of the game. Even Babe Ruth, with no effort to be modest, solemnly averred that Ty Cobb was the greatest ballplayer who ever lived, and Babe pitched against him when Babe himself was at his best on the mound.

Ty Cobb was not a "natural" athlete in the sense that any of his accomplishments came without trying. He owed his eminence to endless practice and indomitable determination. He just would not take second place to anyone, regardless of his natural skills; and if he failed in some effort on the diamond he would practice until he succeeded. Cobb broke into baseball in an age when just staying on the team required brute determination. When he was a rookie, his teammates broke his bats, bumped him aside in batting practice, cut holes in his shoes, and even locked him out of his hotel room. He had to fight for his place on the team and he had to fight to win ball games.

Batting was his special skill. No one in the American League ever earned a higher batting average than he did and only one man (George Sisler) equaled his high mark of .420, which Cobb made in 1911. But hitting safely was not just a matter of meeting the ball with the bat. It required careful placing of the ball sometimes, a fast start, and often a determined slide. Although he threw right-handed Cobb batted left-handed because it put him closer to first. He held his hands well apart on the bat so he could adjust to the pitch and to the strategic situation. If the infielders played him close, he might slap the ball past them. If they played him deep, he would dump the ball in front of them and beat the throw. If a

When Ty Cobb
came to Detroit
he had to
fight for his
turn in batting
practice.

Ty Cobb sometimes
played first base. Here
he wears a first-baseman's
glove and carries
an outfielder's.

Cobb roars into
base (above) while fielder
leaps for his life.

pitch was too far outside, and the situation required a hit, he might throw his bat at the ball and still hit it safely.

On the baselines he was a terror. He kept his spikes sharp, not merely to frighten or slash the opposing basemen (as some people said) but because sharp spikes meant better footing and a quicker start. He studied pitchers until he knew just when he could get the jump on a pitch. He slid into a base fearlessly and sometimes deliberately kicked a ball out of a waiting glove, or knocked a baseman loose from it. He allowed no one the right to stand between him and the base he wanted.

As a batter, he led the American League 12 times; and he led the league six times in stolen bases. He holds the American League record in games played, times at bat, total runs scored, stolen bases, total hits, and total three-base hits (the type of hit that best indicates speed on the basepaths and the willingness to try for that extra base). In 1922, when he had been in the big leagues 17 years, he four times made 5 hits in one game—a modern record. On May 5, 1925, he made 6 hits in 6 times at bat. In 1915, he made the league record for stolen bases: 96. His lifetime batting average, the highest of any Hall-of-Famer, was .367.

As a manager, Cobb was most successful in teaching his batting tricks to others. Harry Heilmann, the great right-handed batter, credited Cobb with making a batting champion out of him.

Cobb, after a season in the bushes, spent 22 seasons with the Detroit Tigers, then ended his career, at the age of 41, by hitting .323 in 95 games with the Philadelphia Athletics. He remained close to the game all his life and gave frequent advice on player deals to George Weiss, the great builder of the New York Yankees and Cobb's lifelong friend.

An outfielder all through his career, Cobb usually played first base in exhibition games, once played second base for Detroit, and in 1925, when he was managing Detroit, actually pitched a game (to no decision).

# EDWARD TROWBRIDGE COLLINS second

baseman in Connie Mack's famous $100,000 infield, shares

with Bobby Wallace a record for consecutive years as an active player in the major leagues: 25. He started playing professional baseball when he was still attending Columbia University, and he played his first game with the Philadelphia Athletics when he had just turned 19. He went to bat only 15 times that season (1906) and got but 3 hits. In 1907, he played part of the year in Philadelphia and then played 4 games with Newark, in the Eastern League. In 1908, he was back with Connie Mack's Athletics to stay until 1914, when he was sold to the Chicago White Sox. After 12 seasons there, he returned to the Athletics to finish his active career.

Eddie Collins is still considered by many authorities the best defensive second baseman the game ever saw. But he was a great hitter and runner too. He had a lifetime average of .333 with a high mark (in 1920) of .369. In 1910 and in 1919 he led the league in stolen bases and he still holds the modern record of 6 bases stolen in 1 game. He did this twice in the same year: September 11 and 22, 1912.

Another baseball art that Collins was a master of was stealing signs and "reading" pitchers. He made a full-time study of the pitchers he faced, searching for the telltale movements that would foretell the curve, or the fast ball, or the pitch-out —or the pick-off throw. Because of this ability to decipher the opponents, Collins was an expert on the hit-and-run play, on the drag bunt (he batted left-handed), and on the squeeze. His 509 sacrifice hits is a record. He is also one of the few players ever to make 3000 base hits in the major leagues.

His ability to remember the idiosyncrasies of opposing players served Collins well in the field too. He never seemed to make any diving stops or wild dashes, yet he was always on the spot when the ball came along and could receive and get rid of the ball in the pivot of a double play faster than any man of his day. He himself had only one major idiosyncrasy: a habit of sticking a wad of chewing gum on the button of his cap and popping it into his mouth if the pitcher got 2 strikes on him. They very seldom got the third.

# SAMUEL EARL CRAWFORD called Wahoo Sam

because he was born in Wahoo, Nebraska, made more three-

Harry Heilmann used Cobb style at bat.
Eddie Collins, right, played 25 years.
Sam Crawford came from Wahoo, Neb.

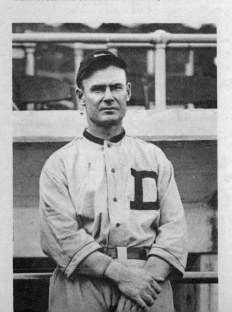

base hits in his big-league career than any other man who ever played. In his 4 years in the National League, Sam hit 62, and in his 15 years in the American League he hit 250.

A tall, solid young man, with oversize hands and feet, Sam Crawford gave up a barbering career and made the big leagues almost as soon as he tried. Sam's greatest fame came to him in Detroit, where he landed in 1903 after a peace settlement between the National League and the American League separated him from Cincinnati and awarded him to Detroit. (He had signed contracts with both.) Sam, who played left field and batted left-handed, immediately began to slash his long long hits to right and right-center, where they had plenty of room to roll.

Sam Crawford, along with Ty Cobb and Bobby Veach, made up Detroit's dream outfield in the pre-Babe Ruth era. All were fast, all three hit solidly, all stole bases well, and they played together as if they operated on the same strings. But Sam was finished in the big leagues before his partners wore out, for he had started a good deal sooner. After 1917, he found room for himself in the Pacific Coast League, where, at the age of 41, he was still pounding the ball for an average of .318.

# ELMER HARRISON FLICK is remembered chiefly

because he led the American League 1 season (1905) with the lowest average that ever took the championship: .306. Yet he often hit for a far higher average than that. In 1900, with the Philadelphia Nationals, he hit .378. And in the minor leagues, with Dayton, he had hit .386 in 1897. He was a small solid man who, like Ty Cobb, hit from the left-handers' side of the plate, even though he threw right-handed. Like all hitters who are fast afoot, he specialized in 3-baggers, leading the league in triples for 3 successive years (1905-6-7).

In 1906 the Detroit Tigers, annoyed by the quarrelsome manners of their rookie outfielder, offered to trade Ty Cobb even-up for Elmer Flick. But the Cleveland management would have none of it. Flick was a bread-and-butter man for them, while Cobb seemed headed for a short career. But Flick suddenly developed ulcers, or some other severe stomach trouble, and began to fade badly. In 1908 he could play in only 9 games. He tried again in 1909, when he got into 66 games. In 1910 he played but 24 and then the Cleveland management reluctantly gave up on their dynamic little star. The next year, with Toledo of the American Association, he staged a sort of comeback, getting into 84 games and batting .326. In 1912, he played even more, but his hitting had fallen off badly and he had to face the fact that he was finished.

Elmer had started in organized baseball with Youngstown of the Interstate League, when he was just turned 20. He put in a year with Youngstown and a year with Dayton before the Philadelphia Nationals signed him in 1898. He spent 4 seasons in Philadelphia, pounding the ball with great authority, before he jumped to Cleveland in May 1902.

In the American League Flick exhibited both speed and power. He led the league in stolen bases in 1904 with 42, and he led again in 1906 with 39, tying with Anderson of Washington. He did not seem therefore like any less than a match for Cobb until 1908, when Cobb began to blaze away on the baselines and Flick, crippled by his stomach trouble (which some observers blamed on "the water at New Orleans"), began to weaken.

Flick was not nearly as big a man as Cobb. He stood 5 feet 8 and weighed only 160 pounds. But if his health had not given out there are those who say he would have lasted as long as the Georgia Peach, and have left a good many records of his own.

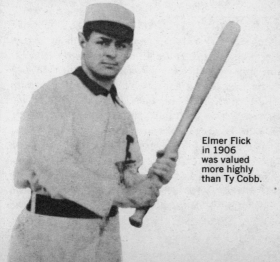

Elmer Flick
in 1906
was valued
more highly
than Ty Cobb.

# BURLEIGH ARLAND GRIMES, the last of the

legal spitballers, was a tough, aggressive player and a husky right-hander. He actually did not use the spitball as often as batters thought he did. He often bluffed so they always looked for it.

Grimes started his big-league career in 1916 with Pittsburgh, and after an unimpressive beginning he moved to the Brooklyn Dodgers in 1918 and became a star. In his first year with the Dodgers he won 19 games. He reached his top when he was with Pittsburgh in 1928, winning 25 games while losing 14. His highest percentage was reached the following year with Pittsburgh, when he won 17 and lost 7 for a percentage of .708.

Grimes won the first World Series game he ever pitched, —a game against Cleveland in 1920. He got into another World Series in 1930 when he was with St. Louis and lost the first game in that series to the Athletics, 5 to 2. He got his revenge the following year when he held the Athletics to 2 hits in the third game of the World Series and beat the man who had trimmed him twice previously — Lefty Bob Grove. He also won the seventh game in that series, beating Earnshaw 4 to 2. Burleigh was traded to Chicago then and appeared in the 1932 World Series against the Yankees. In 1934, he ended his career and in 1937 returned to the majors to manage the Dodgers for two years.

# HARRY EDWIN HEILMANN was a good hitter when

he came up to the Detroit Tigers from Portland of the Northwestern League in 1914, but he did not become a great hitter until after he had put in a season with San Francisco in the Coast League and had played 4 more seasons with Detroit. Then suddenly he began to pound out hits at the rate of almost 2 in every 5 times at bat. The difference, he said, was that Ty Cobb, his teammate at Detroit, became manager of the team and decided to show the young man how to get base hits. Before Cobb took over, Harry's best season batting average had been .320. The first year under Ty's direction (1921) Harry hit .394 and led the American League. In 1923, he led again with .403. In 1925, he led

A determined competitor, Burleigh Grimes'
grim concentration intimidated many batters.

with .393, and in 1927, he came in first again with .398.
Harry played first base, outfield, and a few games at second.
He never batted below .300 after 1919.

What Cobb did, Heilmann said, was to teach him to put
a little more weight on his front foot, to keep his arms away
from his body and his elbows high — routine advice to hitters
nowadays. But Cobb also taught big Harry (he was a 6-feet-1,
200-pound right-hander) to make a study of catchers, who
often called for the same pitch in certain circumstances, and
to learn what to expect. Cobb taught him to imitate Cobb's
stance — crouching so as to shorten the strike zone, keeping
his feet together, gripping the bat with his hands a few inches
apart. Heilmann learned quickly and developed in one season
into one of the greatest hitters in the game.

**MILLER JAMES HUGGINS** was a lead-off batter and an alert fielder who batted over .300 in a full season once in 1912, with the St. Louis Cardinals when his average in 120 games was .304.

Five-foot, four Miller won his place in the Hall as a manager. In 12 seasons with the Yankees beginning in 1918, Huggins won 6 pennants and twice brought his team in second.

Huggins was working with a set of the most wildly individualistic stars ever put on one team. But he won their respect, and eventually their deep affection. He insisted on a strictly business attitude during the game and would not tolerate horseplay while a game was in progress.

Huggins was the manager who first had to discipline the mighty Babe Ruth, and Ruth expressed scorn and disdain for the little fellow at first. But long before Huggins died, Ruth had become devoted to him and he was the only ballplayer to attend him on his deathbed.

Huggins began his professional career with the Cincinnati Reds in 1904, joined the St. Louis Cardinals in 1910 and stayed in baseball until his death at the age of 50 in 1929. As playing manager of the Cards in 1914, Huggins brought them in third, their highest finish since the league was founded in 1876.

Huggins won six pennants for the N. Y. Yankees.

Walter Johnson had fastest pitch ever seen.

# WALTER PERRY JOHNSON

many baseball men will insist, threw a baseball faster than any other pitcher who ever made the major leagues. There was no machine to measure a pitcher's speed in his day; but Johnson left records that are still unmatched. He pitched more American League games than anyone else, 802, and won more, 416. He set a record by pitching 3 successive complete games (September 4, 5, and 7, 1908) and winning them all by shutout. He also set the record for total shutouts: 113; and for consecutive shutout innings: 56. In his 21-year career with Washington, however, he pitched but 1 no-hit game (an error kept it from being perfect).

Johnson's speed used to make batters and umpires blink in amazement. As a kid in the semi-pro ranks he had trouble finding a catcher to hold him. When he got his full growth (6 feet 1 and 200 pounds) he fired the ball past the batter so fast that many a player would pray he would not have to stand up to him again. He had a terror of injuring a man with his speed and would never deliberately throw at a batter.

One reason Johnson lasted in the big leagues so long (he won 23 games for Washington in his 18th year in the big leagues and 20 games the following year, when he was going on 37 years old) was that he paced himself carefully. With 2 strikes and no balls on a batter he liked to experiment with his curve, which hardly curved at all. And when he had a comfortable lead, he did not fret over men getting on base. Usually, when he really had to, he could bear down hard, and he often struck out the side. He had excellent control and an easy, half-sidearm motion. In his best season (1913) he pitched 51 games, won 36 of them and lost only 7, leading the league. He had 12 seasons in which he won 20 or more games, and 2 in which he won more than 30.

A gentle, high-minded, abstemious and friendly man, Johnson had a thousand friends in baseball. He had two nicknames—Big Train, from the whistling speed of his fast ball, and Barney, because he was supposed to drive his car like Barney Oldfield, the racing driver. But in letters to his friends he always signed himself "Walter."

**NAPOLEON LAJOIE** nicknamed Larry, does not own the records that some other hitters do, although he three times led the American League in batting. But his right-handed swing was so smooth and so accurate that many pitchers felt he had no batting weakness at all. He could hit to any field, hit for distance, or bunt to get on base, and in one game, when a pitcher was trying to walk him, he three times reached out one-handed and hit doubles to right field.

As a fielder, Lajoie was one of the finest—on a par with Honus Wagner. His record of 988 fielding chances accepted in a season is the high mark for second basemen in the American League. In 1899, while with the Philadelphia Nationals, he set a mark of 11 putouts in 1 game. In everything he did Larry was noted for his grace. 6 feet 1, weighing almost 200 pounds, Larry, in the infield, was lithe as a cat. At the plate, he was confident, smooth, always the picture hitter. On the basepaths, he stretched many a hit into a double, and long held the record for two-base hits in the American League.

Lajoie had 21 active seasons in the major leagues and left a lifetime batting mark of .339. He finished his baseball career in the minor leagues—with Toronto (where, as manager, he won the only pennant of his career), then with Indianapolis. When he could no longer swing his bat successfully in organized ball he turned to golf, and became a top performer.

**THEODORE AMAR LYONS** like Walter Johnson and Mel Ott, spent his entire big-league career with one club and never played in the minors. Ted's club was the Chicago White Sox, whom he joined when he was 22 and where he became manager at the age of 45. In between he did a lot of pitching. For 11 successive seasons he never appeared in fewer than 40 games and in 3 seasons he worked in 50 or more.

In the beginning, Ted was a fast-ball pitcher who could overpower the strong batters. In his first 8 seasons with the White Sox, Ted had 3 seasons in which he won over 20 games, despite the fact that his team dwelt almost permanently in the second division. In the spring of 1931, his ninth season with Chicago, Ted injured his arm so severely that he was never able to attain again the speed he had known as a youth. That year, although he appeared in 42 games, he won but 4 while losing 6, and he never again achieved the 20-victory mark. Yet he continued to pitch for 12 more seasons—and undoubtedly could have made it 15 if he had not taken 3 seasons out with the Marines in World War II.

The secret of Ted's lasting power was his determined acquisition of a knuckle ball, which he practiced sedulously until he could control it. His ability to keep batters off balance with this tantalizing slow pitch, or with a medium change of pace, enabled him to work without undue strain on his injured muscles.

Napoleon Lajoie hit to any field.
Ted Lyons (right), lasted 21 seasons.
Walter Johnson won 416 games.

# HENRY EMMETT (HEINIE) MANUSH, born in

Tuscumbia, Alabama, was the seventh baseball player born into his family, and the best of them all.

A big left-hander, Heinie was a member of the most murderous outfield ever put together—the Detroit outfield of Cobb, Heilmann, Manush and Fothergill, the back-up man. In 136 games for Detroit in 1926, Heinie's average was .378. Two years later with the St. Louis Browns, Heinie posted the same figure. His lifetime average is .330. His .378 average in 1926 won the league batting crown and he stayed among the batting leaders for 8 years more. In 1928 he and Lou Gehrig led the league in doubles with 47 apiece.

After leaving Detroit, Heinie played with St. Louis and then with Washington, where he stayed 5 seasons. At the age of 35, when his average had fallen off to .273, Heinie was traded to the Red Sox, who kept him one season and then swapped him off to Brooklyn, in the other league. Heinie promptly celebrated his arrival in the curve-ball league by hitting .333 in 132 games. He ended his active career with Pittsburgh in 1939.

Starting with a mining-company team in Utah at the age of 17 and progressing through the minor-league club in Edmonton, Alberta, Heinie spent 22 years as an active ballplayer, then put in a long spell as minor-league manager and big-league scout and coach.

Manush ended his playing days with a lifetime average of .330.

Shortstop of 1914 Miracle Braves was Rabbit Maranville.

118

# WALTER JAMES VINCENT MARANVILLE

called Rabbit, was one of the smallest men ever to play in the big leagues (5 feet 5, and 155 pounds). He was also one of the best liked and one of the funniest. Even his favorite trick of catching a ball with both hands held high against his body—his vest-pocket catch, he called it—seemed like a comedy stunt, for Rab was always doing something to make people laugh. (Once he waded into a hotel pool, caught a goldfish, and took a bite out of it.) But the catch was an important part of his repertoire. He had small hands and wanted to be sure he held on to the ball.

Rabbit was a lion-hearted young man, fast, sure-footed, and aggressive. Before he joined the minor-league team in New Bedford in 1911, young Maranville had played school and sandlot ball as a catcher in Springfield, Massachusetts. He entered organized ball when he was 19 years old and kept on playing until he was 43. Some people say that if he had not broken his leg while sliding home in a spring exhibition game in 1934, he'd be playing yet.

The fans in New Bedford named Maranville Rabbit because of the way he hopped about the infield to collar ground balls. No great man at the plate, he was a fearless and timely hitter who often came through in the clutch. When he moved up to Boston, he joined the team that was to become the Miracle Team in 1914, when Manager George Stallings (with lots of help from Maranville and Johnny Evers) moved them from last place to first place and cleaned up the World Series in 4 straight games.

Maranville starred because he, like Evers, was a team player. He was not out to make records but to win. He had enjoyed the company of ballplayers all his life and he wanted to stay in baseball forever.

Maranville played his final baseball games in 1939, when he was 47, for Albany in the Eastern League, which he managed for a season, and although he had slowed down on the field he was just as aggressive and just as full of fun as when he once crawled between Umpire Hank O'Day's legs at Braves Field to get to the plate.

Eppa Rixey (above),
won 266 games
in twenty years.

Plank (right), had
20 wins or more in eight
seasons out of 17.

Ray Schalk (below),
was thought too small
to be a catcher.

# EDWARD STEWART PLANK the great left-

hander for Connie Mack's Philadelphia Athletics who won 20 or more games for 8 seasons, never pitched in a minor league. He was a grown man before he went to college and it was while he was at Gettysburg College that he discovered he was a pitcher. (As a boy, the story has it, he amused himself by knocking birds off fences by throwing stones and thus developed the strength and control he needed.) When he joined Connie Mack, he was going on 26 years old. But he stayed with Connie for 14 years, then put in a season with St. Louis in the Federal League and 2 seasons with the St. Louis American League entry.

A solemn man who was accused by sports writers of having no sense of humor, Eddie Plank was the slowest-working pitcher of his day. He would spend so much time between pitches, adjusting his cap, hitching his belt, kicking pebbles out of his way, and then going into a rocker motion that might last a half a minute before he let the ball go toward the plate, that many a batter simply could not keep staring at the mound so long. Then, by the time the ball came down, he failed to focus on it.

Eddie's best season with the Athletics was his twelfth, when he was 37 years old. That year, 1912, he won 26 games and lost but 6. He had 5 shutouts. He had won 26 games in 1904 but lost 17 that year. Eddie was a hard-luck pitcher in many ways, for he lost an unusually large number of close games.

# EPPA (JEPTHA) RIXEY was playing for the Cul-

pepper (Virginia) Hurricanes at the age of 7; everyone called him "Eppa" or "Junior." He never heard the name "Jeptha" until he was a grown man pitching in the major leagues, and a newspaperman presented him with it. Eppa liked it so well he adopted it for a middle name.

Eppa, who grew into an enormous young man (6 feet 5 and over 200 pounds), stepped right from the University of Virginia to the roster of the Philadelphia Phillies in 1912. A National League umpire, Charles Rigler, was impressed by the young left-hander's speed and made the deal that brought him into the majors. (It also brought an end to any scouting by umpires, as the other clubs protested.)

Eppa had some trouble at the start, although he won 10 games his first year. In 1913, he won 9 games while losing 5, but the next year he won only 2 while losing 11. In 1915 a new manager, catcher Pat Moran, took over the Phillies, approved of his strong-armed left hander, and helped get him on the track. In 1915, while the Phillies were winning the pennant, Eppa contributed 11 victories. In 1916 he won 22 and lost 10. He was 16 and 21, in a losing cause, in 1917. He entered the army then and served overseas. On his return, he picked up his work-horse chores. But Pat Moran, to whom he gave credit for his development, moved on to Cincinnati and Eppa began to slip. In 1919 he won but 6 games. Next year he won 11 but lost twice as many (he appeared in 43 games). Then he went to Cincinnati and celebrated his reunion with Pat Moran by winning steadily season after season: 19 in 1921; 25 in 1922; 20 in 1923. Indeed, big Eppa did not post a losing season in Cincinnati until 1929, when he was 38 years old. That year, appearing in 35 games, he won 10 and lost 13. He pitched less and less after that—and complained that he was not getting enough work. After a 5 and 5 season in 1932, he finally managed another winning season with a record of 6 won and 3 lost. Then Eppa called it a career and went to selling insurance, a business in which he prospered. His record of 266 victories stood as the best ever attained by a major league left-hander, until Warren Spahn broke it in 1959.

Eppa's fame never matched his skill, perhaps because he never became a World Series hero. In his only World Series game in 1915 he lost to the Boston Red Sox by 1 run, after Harry Hopper, who had hit only 2 home runs all year, bounced 2 lucky homers into the temporary stands in Philadelphia. But Eppa never felt that he was mistreated or ignored by baseball writers or the record keepers. When he was told of his election to the Hall of Fame, he chuckled: "They're really scraping the bottom of the barrel, aren't they?"

Tris Speaker was keystone
in Red Sox dream outfield of
1910-1915. He might
have played for
Pittsburgh if he hadn't
smoked cigarettes.

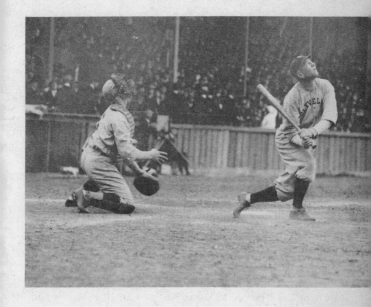

In 1916 Speaker was
sold to Cleveland and became
manager in 1919.

**RAYMOND WILLIAM SCHALK** who played for the Chicago White Sox for 17 seasons, never batted over .286 for them except in his final year as a player, when he went to bat twice and got 2 hits, for an average of 1.000. But he was an iron-man catcher and the ablest fielder of his time in the behind-the-bat position. No other American League catcher ever earned a better fielding percentage. Ray caught in 100 games or more for 12 seasons, 11 of them in a row.

Schalk was a little fellow — 5 feet 7, weighing 155 pounds — but he could move around in his position as no one else has before or since. He shares with Bill Dickey the catcher's league record of 3 assists in an inning — and he has one mark that is strictly his own: he made a putout at one time or other at every base — first, second, third, and home. That is because he was always in on every play and ready to move to any part of the field to stay with the ball.

When Schalk joined the White Sox in 1912, after a season with Taylorville and part of one with Milwaukee, Big Ed Walsh, the Chicago spitballer, refused to believe that tiny Schalk could hold his pitches. But Schalk suggested they warm up together and from that time forth, Big Ed wanted no other catcher. "Too small" to block the plate against the husky runners of his day, Schalk developed a method of sending them spinning off his shinguards that was just as effective.

Ray started to play ball when he was invited to catch for the town team in Litchfield, Illinois. He started to play professionally when he was 18 and joined the White Sox when he was 19. He stayed with them until he was 36, serving as manager in his last 2 seasons. He then played a few games for New York, stacking up a record lifetime total (up to his day) of 1721 games as a catcher, and another 30 or so in which he appeared as pinch-hitter.

**TRISTRAM E. SPEAKER** although hitting was his specialty, was also one of the greatest glove men ever to play center field for a major league team. With the aid of his teammate, Old Cy Young, the Boston pitcher, Speaker practiced hour after hour in the outfield until he learned to tell, by the sound of the bat meeting the ball, and by the timing of Cy Young's swing, just about where the ball was going to fall. With this skill added to his lightning speed, he became a magician in the outfield. He played sometimes almost behind second base and no one has ever matched him in ability to turn his back to the plate and take a fly ball over his shoulder, going away. More than once he robbed hitters of what seemed like certain home runs, once leaping right into the crowd with his back to the diamond and plucking the ball out of the air before he fell into the stands. He tied the American League record for outfield assists (35) in 1909 and tied it again in 1912. There was no such thing as a Texas League single when a big Texan named Speaker was roaming the shallow outfield. He made 2 unassisted double plays in 1918, tying the record.

As a hitter, Spoke led the American League only once, in 1916, after he had been sold to Cleveland because he refused to take a salary cut. That year he batted .386. Most of the time he ran close behind a man named Ty Cobb, who became his close friend and eventually his teammate. Spoke made 11 hits in a row on July 8, 9, and 10 in 1920. And when he completed his career he had set a new mark for two-base hits in the major leagues: 793.

Tris Speaker became manager of the Cleveland Indians in 1919 and held the job until 1926, when he resigned to go first to Washington, then to Philadelphia, and finally to Newark in the International League, where he managed for a season and a half. He led his Cleveland team to only 1 pennant, in 1920, and he took the World Series too, making 8 hits in that Series himself.

**JOHN PETER WAGNER** is still placed near the top of the list of all-time All-Stars. In his day, a baseball fan could always start an argument on the subject of whether Ty Cobb or Honus Wagner was the greatest ballplayer alive. Nowadays nearly everyone will name Cobb but in the early 1900's the competition was close. Honus was certainly the greatest shortstop of his era. He could range the whole distance from the deep hole near third to right behind second base to dig ground balls out of the gravel and hurl them (often with a handful of

Honus Wagner was best shortstop of his day.

dirt flying along) hard and fast to first base. Very few men in baseball ever owned a stronger arm than Wagner did and in this department at least he was far ahead of Cobb.

Wagner had an extraordinary pair of hands, with fingers as long as the whole hand of a small man, dangling, some people said, like a bunch of bananas. When he gripped a baseball, the ball looked like a button. Bowlegged as he was, he could fly on the basepaths and on defense he could stand up to the toughest of them. Even the hard-boiled Orioles learned to give the big Dutchman room when he came cannonading down the basepaths. And Ty Cobb once told ruefully of a day when he warned big Honus, "I'm coming down on the next pitch!" This warning, which usually unnerved lesser men, just made Wagner more determined and when Cobb slid in, spikes high, there was Honus to lay the hard side of the ball on his face. "He split my lip for me," said Cobb admiringly.

This was during the only Series when the two great stars played against each other—the World Series of 1909. In that Series Wagner (and Pittsburgh) ran off with the victory. While Cobb stole only 1 base and batted .231, Wagner stole 6 bases and batted .333. (In his first World Series, against Boston, in 1903, Wagner too had been a disappointment, with an average of only .214.)

Wagner started in organized baseball comparatively late in life. He was 21 years old when he broke in with Steubenville, Ohio. His older brother was already a professional ballplayer but Honus had played only as a semi-pro, making his living meanwhile at the coal mines near his home in Carnegie, Pennsylvania. He started out in baseball as a pitcher but gave the job up quickly. "I used to strike out half the side," he would explain (with forgivable exaggeration), "and walk the other half." He played the outfield and infield with equal skill, and played them both in 1895, when he worked with 3 different minor league teams, besides Steubenville: Mansfield, in the Ohio State League; Adrian, in the Michigan State League; and Warren, in the Iron-Oil League.

Ed Barrow bought Wagner from Steubenville in 1896 and took him to play for Paterson, New Jersey, in the Atlantic League. In mid-season, 1897, Wagner was sold to Louisville

Chicago's Big Ed Walsh was
greatest of the spitballers.

Big hands on Wagner (left),
could hide a baseball.

Zack Wheat hit .375 two
seasons in a row, 1923-24.

131

and was transferred, with the best of that team, to Pittsburgh when Louisville dropped out of the National League in 1900. In all his time in the minors, and for his first 17 years in the majors Wagner never owned a batting average of less than .300. Nor did he ever, in the minors or in the majors, until he was 42 years old, play less than 100 games a year. He led the National League in batting eight times—four times in a row (1906-9). He set the National League lifetime mark of games played (2785) and is one of the small group of men who gathered over 3000 hits. As a base stealer, he ranks fourth behind Cobb, Eddie Collins, and Max Carey, in modern lifetime totals.

After he began to slow down a little (he was troubled by rheumatic pains even in his best years), Wagner became manager of Pittsburgh but he resigned after three days. That year, 1917, was his 21st year in the majors and his last as an active player, although he did play some semi-pro ball in Pittsburgh for years afterward. He came back to the Pirates as a coach in 1933 and remained there until his death.

# EDWARD AUGUSTIN WALSH was a spitballer,

and probably the best of them all. A big strong right-hander who never seemed to tire, big Ed was willing to pitch every game if he was asked. In 1908, with the Chicago White Sox, he worked in 66 games and won 40 of them. That year he led all the pitchers in the league, pitched the most shutouts, and scored the most strikeouts. He also set the all-time record for innings pitched in one season: 464. And he pitched 3 successive complete games on the schedule, 2 of them on 1 day. He won that double-header, then pitched the next game on the schedule and lost it, although he struck out 15 batters, walked one, and allowed but 4 hits. The very next day, Ed came in as relief pitcher, struck out Lajoie with the bases full, and saved the game.

Ed had won another double-header in 1905 and pitched a no-hit game against Boston in 1911. In his only World Series (the all-Chicago series of 1906) Ed pitched 2 games and won them both, fanning 12 batters in 1 game, and yielding a 2-game total of 8 hits.

132

Born in Pennsylvania, Ed first played organized ball with Wilkes-Barre in the Pennsylvania State League. He did not realize his full potential as a pitcher until he began to use the spitball, in 1906. The next year he won 24 games for Chicago and, after his 40-victory year in 1908, hit a high mark again with 27 wins in 1911. In 1914, his mighty arm gave out.

# ZACHARY DAVIS WHEAT the best outfielder

the Brooklyn Dodgers ever owned, was a fleet-footed and sure-handed young man, raised on a farm in Texas and built rangy and strong as a horse. He was a solid hitter who accomplished more with his bat than any other man who ever graced the Brooklyn roster. He leads all Brooklynites in games played, in times at bat, in total hits, in singles, in doubles, in triples, and in total bases. In 1918, he led the National League in batting with an average of .335. (His top mark was .375, achieved in successive years, 1923 and 1924.) In 1916 he hit safely in 29 consecutive games.

But Zach, also called Buck, was at his best in the outfield. Speeding all over left field on his tiny feet (he wore a size 6 shoe), he specialized in snaring line drives by reaching across his body and taking them backhanded.

Zach started as a professional with Fort Worth in the Texas League when he was almost 19. He played with Shreveport in the Texas League, and with Mobile in the Southern League before he finally came up to Brooklyn in 1909. He did not hit .300 in the minors but as soon as he got to Brooklyn he started to and in the 18 seasons he played there, he hit .300 or better 13 times. He was a left-handed batter, not especially adept at getting down to first at top speed. But once past first he could fly, and he more often than not was able to grab that extra base.

Zack Wheat was Brooklyn's favorite outfielder for 18 seasons: 1909-26.

# THE GOLDEN AGE

Babe Ruth called his shot in World Series with Cubs, 1932. Here he crosses plate after hitting home run right where he said he would. Lou Gehrig, next at bat, offers Babe congratulations.

BASEBALL HAD ITS GOLDEN AGE BETWEEN THE WORLD WARS. THE ERA OF THE MILLION-DOLLAR OPERATION WAS DOMINATED BY BABE RUTH, NEW LINE-UPS OF HIGHLY-PAID PLAYERS AND MODERN STADIUMS FILLED WITH CAPACITY CROWDS. UNDER THE CONTROL OF A NATIONAL COMMISSIONER, BASEBALL OUTGREW THE LAST VESTIGES OF ITS ROWDY PAST.

# GROVER CLEVELAND ALEXANDER known

throughout baseball as Old Pete, tied Christy Mathewson in winning more games than any other National League pitcher who ever lived: 373. In three seasons (1915-17), Old Pete won 31, 33, and 30 games for the Philadelphia Nationals. Then he was traded to the Chicago Cubs and he never had a losing season there. In 1920, his tenth season in the major leagues, he appeared in 46 games for Chicago and won 27.

Although Old Pete spent 20 seasons in the majors with Philadelphia, Chicago, St. Louis, and back in Philadelphia again, and won more than 20 games in 9 of those seasons, he is still remembered best for his relief pitching for the St. Louis Cardinals in the seventh game of the 1926 World Series against the Yankees. Alexander had won the sixth game and, at the age of 39, seemed to have completed his chores. But Manager Hornsby called him in to relieve Jess Haines, who had a blister on his finger, in the seventh inning of the seventh game, with the bases full and Tony Lazzeri at bat. Lazzeri got one blazing foul off Alexander that landed in the left-field stands, just a few feet out of home-run territory. Then Alexander fanned him and went on to save the game and the series. Alexander struck out 2199 men in his major league career, yet this is the one strikeout that is remembered.

No pitcher has ever matched Old Pete's record of 28 victories in his first major league season. Nor has anyone exceeded his record of 16 shutouts in a season. He twice won both ends of double-headers and he posted 21 victories for St. Louis in 1927, the year he turned 40. A master of control and an efficient workman on the mound, Old Pete once completed a major league game in 2 minutes under an hour.

# LUCIUS BENJAMIN (LUKE) APPLING is the

only shortstop who ever led the American League in batting. And he did it twice—in 1936 with an average of .388 and in 1943 with an average of .328. Luke also played more games at shortstop than any other player in the history of the major leagues. During the 20 years he played with the White Sox, he played shortstop in 2,218 games, made 2,749 hits and appeared as third baseman or pinch hitter in 204 more. But he is remembered today for frequent injuries to himself and for his ability to foul-off pitches by the dozen.

Luke's penchant for fouling-off pitches derived from his habit of punching most of his hits to the opposite field. He tired out many a pitcher that way.

Born in High Point, North Carolina, Luke became a football and baseball star at Oglethorpe University in Atlanta, Ga. He signed with the Atlanta club of the Southern Association and was soon sought after by major-league clubs. At first fans booed him because he booted so many ground balls. But he later showed the fans the best fielding they had ever seen at his position.

Grover Cleveland Alexander won 30 games 3 years in a row.

Appling played more games at short than any player in history.

# GORDON STANLEY COCHRANE a solidly built

young man of medium height, was one of the fastest men ever to crouch behind the bat. He was aggressive, smart, and fiery—a natural leader and a never-say-die competitor. He led the American League six times in total putouts for a catcher; and he hit the ball solidly and often. In 1932, with Philadelphia, he hit 23 home runs. His lifetime batting average was

Frankie Frisch, a tough customer, at 1934 World Series.

Grover Cleveland Alexander, age 40, won 21 games in 1927.

In World War II
Cochrane led
U. S. Navy team
at Great Lakes
Station.

139

.320 and his top mark was .357, attained in 1929. He caught 100 or more games in 11 successive seasons.

Sold to the Detroit Tigers in 1933 for a price in excess of $100,000, Mickey became manager there and led the club to its first pennant in 25 years in 1934. He won another pennant, plus the World Championship, in 1935. His playing career came to an untimely end when he suffered a fractured skull when hit by a pitched ball on May 25, 1937. The previous season, he had spent many weeks on the sidelines, suffering from a succession of injuries and ailments, including trouble with his eyes and stomach. This accident put him off the diamond for good. The following year, when a new owner took over the Tigers, Cochrane was dropped as manager; but he came back in later years to join the Philadelphia Athletics as coach and then to become general manager. In the meantime he served in the Navy during the war and coached a first-rank baseball team for the Great Lakes Naval Training Station.

# JOSEPH EDWARD CRONIN could play almost
any baseball position. During his 20 active seasons in the major leagues, this solid, lantern-jawed Irishman played shortstop, all three bases, and the outfield. Then, to prove that his baseball was not all in his muscles, he served as player-manager, nonplaying manager, general manager, and finally as American League president.

The Washington Senators bought Cronin halfway through the 1928 season. Joe made good, after half a dozen false starts.

In his first full year with Washington, Joe hit .282. That was the lowest mark he made for a complete year in his entire stay with Washington. In 1930, Joe hit .346, the high mark of his career. As a fielder he led all American League shortstops in 1932 and 1933.

Joe, an aggressive yet good-natured man, was a natural field boss, always alert to the play that was in the making, respected by his mates, and an instinctive strategist. After 2 seasons as manager (he won 1 pennant) he was sold (for a quarter million dollars, it was said) to the Boston Red Sox. He managed Boston for 13 seasons.

Joe won only 1 pennant with the Red Sox, in 1946, but he had his team in contention most of the time. Next to the 1946 pennant, Joe is proudest of the time in 1939 when the Red Sox—always the Yankees' bitterest foes, since the Yanks "stole" the entire Red Sox line-up, beginning with Babe Ruth, in the 1920's—took 5 straight from New York.

# JAY HANNA. DEAN called Dizzy, was the son of an itinerant cotton picker. He was a strong right-hander with a fine three-quarter overhand motion. His fast ball smoked and his curve ball (or "crooky" as he called it) seemed to snap its tail in the batter's face. He started playing formalized baseball in the army at Fort Sam Houston, Texas. A train conductor wrote to Branch Rickey of the St. Louis Cardinals about him and Rickey sent a scout to look the boy over. On the basis of the scout's report Rickey invited Dean to a tryout camp, took one look at the 6-feet-3 youngster with the devil-may-care attitude, and signed him to play for St. Joseph. Success came to Dean at once, and almost immediately earned him his nickname, for his behavior in St. Joseph was eccentric enough to delight even the most jaded sports writer. But Dean was no eccentric on the mound. In his first season in organized ball he won 17 games and struck out 134 batters for St. Joseph. He won 30 games for the St. Louis Cardinals in 1934 and 28 in 1935. He set a National League strikeout record for his day of 17 in a game and he led the league in strikeouts 4 seasons in a row. He also shared a minor league hitting record, along with 7 other players: He got 2 base hits in a single inning one day.

An injury shortened Dizzy's career, when he had to change his pitching motion to favor a sore toe hit by a line drive in the 1937 All-Star Game. His arm went lame on him then and he never regained his speed. His cunning kept him in the big leagues, however, for another 3 years. He closed out his career with a flash of glory when in 1947, with the St. Louis American League team, after he had become a highly popular baseball broadcaster, he pitched 4 innings in the final game, allowed no runs and got a hit in his only time at bat.

Joe Cronin (left), was a topnotch tennis player before he joined the Pittsburgh Pirates. They sold him to Washington, where he became a great shortstop and manager.

Left to right are President Roosevelt, Clark Griffith, Washington owner; Joe Cronin, and Giants' Bill Terry.

Dizzy Dean had
seen his best days
when he joined
the Chicago Cubs
in 1938.

But Dean could still fog
the fast one through
often enough to win a few
games for the Cubs.

At right, Dizzy Dean
at the height of his fame:
30-game winner
for St. Louis, 1934.

**WILLIAM MALCOLM DICKEY** never played for any major league club except the New York Yankees, but he did a great deal of catching for them. A long-legged, long-armed, broad-shouldered lad from Arkansas, Dickey was unusually tall for a catcher and had to squat a long way to get down behind the bat.

When Bill joined the Yankees at the age of 20, he had already done a lot of catching in the minors. In 1939, with the Yankees, he caught 140 games, and he holds the record of 13 seasons in which he caught 100 games or more. Bill could hit big-league pitching too. In his first full year with the Yankees, he hit .324. In 16 seasons (with time out for war service) Bill fell below .300 in batting only five times.

Although Bill was not fast on his feet, he was fast-thinking and he was quick to diagnose plays. He pounced on bunts like a cat and blocked the plate without fear. He caught 125 games without a passed ball in 1931 and he shares the major league record for catchers of 3 assists in 1 inning. Six times he led all catchers in putouts and three times in assists. In 1941, he made an unassisted double play.

It was his big bat rather than his steadiness behind the plate that kept Bill in the line-up so often. In 2 consecutive games in 1937 he hit home runs with the bases full. He hit a total of 29 that year. He also set a record (since tied) by making 4 hits in 1 World's Series game (October 5, 1938), and another record by batting in 5 runs in 1 World's Series game (October 2, 1936).

**JOSEPH PAUL DIMAGGIO** the pride of the New York Yankees, might have become the pride of Boston, or some other city, had there been any baseball executive besides George Weiss willing to take a chance on Joe's "bad" knee. But other clubs shied away from Joe after his left knee snapped out of joint one day and forced him to spend 6 weeks on crutches. The Yankee management, however, who had been impressed as everyone else had been by Joe's great play for the San Francisco Seals in the Pacific Coast League, sent Joe to a doctor and received assurance that the injury was not permanent. So Joe became a Yankee and never played for any other major league club.

Starting with the New York Yankees in 1936, after 3 full seasons (and the tail end of another) with the Seals, Joe played 10 full seasons with the Yankees, spent three years in military service and in 1949 played about half the regularly scheduled games. In this year, he was suffering from a recurrence of a bone spur on his heel that had threatened to end his career a year earlier. He was no longer "pulling" the ball in the manner he had made famous. Every time he ran, pain knifed through his foot. Yet he hit .346 that season, collected 14 home runs, and played in all 5 World Series games.

Joe was essentially a long-ball hitter. He had about the widest stance of anyone in the big leagues in his day and strode forward just a few inches when he swung at the pitch. Like most of the great modern sluggers, Joe was a wrist hitter and could wait until the last second before snapping his bat around to drive the ball to deep left. His fielding was a delight to watch, for he covered ground with a smooth loping stride and seemed able to encompass the whole outfield if need be. He had a strong arm, until age and injury weakened it somewhat, and threw many a runner out at the plate from deep center field. The admiration of nearly all his contemporaries, Joe set a style for Yankee outfielders and for Yankee hitters— to perform the job in workmanlike, aggressive, and consistent manner, without flamboyance and without letup, and to play to win.

Joe had a lifetime batting average of .325 and twice led the league in batting averages of .381 (1939) and .352 (1940). His high mark in the minors was .398.

Joe's most famous batting record was his hitting safely in 56 consecutive games, a mark he made in 1941. But in the Pacific Coast League 8 years earlier he had hit safely in 61 consecutive games.

# ROBERT WILLIAM ANDREW FELLER
Cleveland's fireball pitcher, came into the big leagues straight from school, when he was not yet eighteen years old. (The

Bill Dickey of the
Yankees caught over 100
games 13 years in a
row. Note here how fingers
of his "meat" hand are
closed, but relaxed,
to avoid fracture.

New York Murderers' Row,
1936: Dickey, .362;
Gehrig, .354; DiMaggio, .323;
Lazzeri, .287. This was
DiMaggio's first
season; Gehrig's 14th.

Joe DiMaggio
was a pull hitter
with a wide stance and
short stride.

Joe DiMaggio's single scored
three runs this time, thanks to Joe's
miraculous slide, plus two errors.

DiMaggio crosses plate (above) in 45th game of 1941 hitting streak.

Cleveland team gave him a job in the concession department to keep him handy before he was ready to put a uniform on.) Ballplayers who faced him then said he was the fastest man since Johnson and there are even a few who think he might have been a mite faster. Johnson, although a modest man, could not agree that young Bob threw faster than he had thrown; but nearly everyone agreed that Bob was surely next best.

Feller's fast ball, like Johnson's, came down so fast that many a batter lost sight of it and on that account the hitters, during Feller's best years, stood "on top of their spikes" in the batter's box, ready to get out of the way in a hurry. Feller's trick of looking everywhere but at the plate when he was preparing to deliver the ball increased the batters' uneasiness.

Had Feller not lost three full seasons because of his war service, his records might have topped them all, for he was at his best when he joined the Navy, having completed consecutive seasons when he won 24, 27, and 25 games. After the war, in 1946 and 1947, he won 26 and 20 games respectively and in 1948 he helped the Indians win their first pennant in many years by posting 19 victories. Unlike Johnson, Bob Feller had a magnificent curve ball that came down nearly as fast as his hard one. His motion was "big" and loose and overpowering, with a deep pump and a mighty stride that in itself was almost enough to make a hitter quail. On April 16, 1940, Feller opened the season with a no hit 1-0 victory over Chicago, the first no-hit opening day game in the American League since 1900. Six years later, on another cool April day, when he was "not feeling right" he pitched another no-hitter against New York in the Yankee stadium. On October 2, 1938, he broke Rube Waddell's strikeout record by fanning 18 Detroit Tigers in the first game of a double-header. In this game he fanned six batters in a row, to tie the league record. In his first season in organized baseball, he had fanned 16 Red Sox batters during the first game of an August double-header.

In 1946 Feller established the modern season record of 348 strikeouts and for seven seasons he struck out more

Even oldtimers agreed that Bob Feller
was nearly as fast as Walter Johnson.

batters than any other pitcher in the league. Three times (1941-46-47) he led the league in shutouts, twice tied for the lead (1939 and 1940), and in 1940 he topped the league in earned-run average (2.62).

Feller pitched in but one World Series (against Boston in 1948) and could not win a game. In All-Star competition, however, he was nearly invincible. Between 1939 and 1946 he pitched in four All-Star games, a total of 11 innings, and allowed but one earned run.

## JAMES EMORY FOXX despite a friendly, outgoing

nature, was known as "the Beast" in organized baseball, simply because he seemed something more than human at the plate. Not quite 6 feet tall, he had a chest and a pair of arms that would have looked normal on a giant; and he could use the muscles hidden there to rocket a batted ball as far as any human being has ever done before or since.

Jimmy was one of the Philadelphia Athletics' most famous graduates and he was discovered by an older graduate of the same club: Frank "Home Run" Baker. When Baker first saw Foxx, Jimmy was a catcher with Easton (Maryland) in the Eastern Shore League and he was only 16 years old. At Baker's urging, Connie Mack signed Jimmy when the boy was 17, let him go to bat 9 times (during which Jimmy got 6 hits), then put him in Providence to learn some other position besides catcher. Mack already had a catcher named Cochrane. Jimmy learned to play first base and third base and in 1928, at the age of 20, became one of Connie's regulars. He batted .328 that year and got 13 home runs. Not for 14 years did he hit so few home runs again. In 1932, he led the American League with 58 home runs; in 1933, with 48; in 1935 (tie), with 36; and in 1939, with 35. Only Babe Ruth, in his major league career, hit more home runs than Jimmy did. Foxx collected 534.

Jimmy's drives were not long flies. He hit the ball on the nose and drove it straight and hard. (He actually did, in batting practice, hit a young pitcher on the skull with a drive and send the young man out of the big leagues.)

Jimmy Foxx
with the Red Sox
played first,
third, pitcher,
catcher and
outfield.

In 1929, the three sluggers at right, Foxx, Cochrane, and Simmons, won the championship for Connie Mack's A's.

Jimmy Foxx, above, hit 58 homers in 1932 and 50 in 1938.

Frankie Frisch, shown here as
player and manager, graduated from
John McGraw's tough Giants
to lead the St. Louis Gashouse Gang.

Jimmy got at least 1 home run in every World Series he ever played in: with Philadelphia in 1929 (2 home runs), 1930, and 1931. After he was sold to the Boston Red Sox in 1936, Jimmy hit 41 home runs his first season there and 2 seasons later hit 50. He was the American League batting leader in 1933, with .356. He also led the league in 1938, when he was with Boston, with .349. Before he was through, he had played pitcher as well as catcher and had become an able performer at both first and third base. He still holds the record for the number of consecutive years in which a batter hit 30 or more home runs. Jimmy did it 12 times.

# FRANK FRANCIS FRISCH a switch hitter known as

the Fordham Flash, was no college-boy athlete. He was rough-and-ready, aggressive, and tough as they came, cast in the image of John McGraw, a man he greatly admired and the big-league manager he first played for. He was the ideal leader of the team with which he earned his greatest fame—the great St. Louis Gashouse Gang of the 1930's.

While Frankie was with McGraw, he played second base, third base, and shortstop and starred at each position. Eventually he settled to second base, where he was recognized as one of the game's greatest. But right to the end of his active career he was ready to fill in at either of the other spots as well. Frankie was the "holler guy" in the infield—the man who could cajole, encourage, even enrage his teammates to play their best; and he was equally vociferous on the bench, where he took a vocal part in every maneuver on the field.

Although Frankie never led the league in batting, his life-time major league average is .316 and his high mark was .348, made in 1923, with the Giants, when he led the league in total base hits. In 1924, while with the Giants, he once made 6 hits in 6 consecutive times at bat.

Because Frankie ate and slept baseball, he was born to be a manager. He took charge both on the field and off—and sometimes after he had been banished from the field. (A favorite trick, when he was manager and had been ordered from the field for overenthusiastic protests, was to lie flat on the dugout floor and run the team from there.)

Henry Louis Gehrig,
Yankee Iron Horse,
played in 2,130
consecutive games.

Lou Gehrig here is wearing the uniform of his "Larrupin Lous," barnstorming team that toured with Ruth's "Bustin Babes."

Lou Gehrig wept when
60,000 fans cheered him in his
final appearance, 1939.

Above, Gehrig makes
a putout on Joe Vosmik
in June, 1936.

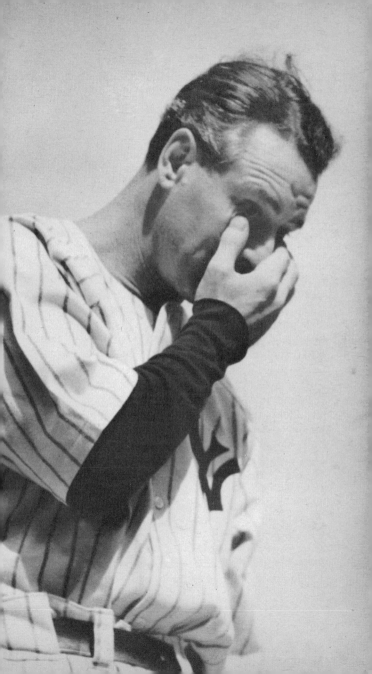

Frank was a shortstop at Fordham and while he was at college played shortstop for the New York Athletic Club every Sunday. He was signed by McGraw while still in college and never played in the minors. It was McGraw who discovered he could play second and third better than short and it was McGraw who instilled the win-the-game-if-it-kills-you spirit in the youngster.

Frankie three times led the National League in stolen bases. He played in 8 World Series, 4 with New York and 4 with St. Louis. In his 2 All-Star Games, he made 4 hits in 7 times at bat.

# HENRY LOUIS GEHRIG played more games in a row (for the New York Yankees) than anyone in major league baseball. Lou, who was given nicknames that never stuck (Larrupin' Lou, Buster) was finally called, in print at least, the Iron Horse, for he seemed indestructible. Despite colds, bruises, pains, aches, and even despite the crippling disease that finally killed him, Lou Gehrig put his uniform on and at least made an appearance in more consecutive games than most people ever see: 2130.

A big, rugged, quiet, and determined man, Lou began to play first base regularly for the New York Yankees on June 1, 1925 and did not leave the starting line-up until May 2, 1939, when he took himself out of the game because he was too ill to play ever again. He died 2 years later. Because he was Babe Ruth's teammate, he seemed always to be coming in second to Ruth and never achieved quite the headlines that Babe did. But his batting feats were nearly as miraculous. Five times he hit more than 40 home runs in a season and twice led the league with 49. He hit 4 home runs in 3 consecutive World Series games against St. Louis in 1928. He set an American League record for most runs batted in (184) in a single season. He hit 4 consecutive home runs in 1 game on June 3, 1932; and he set a major league lifetime record for most home runs with the bases full: 23. He led the American League in batting in 1934 with a mark of .363.

Gehrig signed with New York in 1923 and was farmed to

Hartford for most of the next 2 seasons. Then Lou moved in at first base and hit 20 home runs and batted .295. His average did not fall below .300 again until 1938, when he hit .295 again. In this, his last full season in the game, he hit 29 home runs.

A legend before he left the game, and a full-blown hero afterward, Lou has a street named after him in New York, where he had been a high-school football player as a boy.

# CHARLES GEHRINGER who played second base for
the Detroit Tigers for 16 full seasons and part of 3 more, became known as "the Mechanical Man" because he always did his work the same way—perfectly. A quiet young man from a farm near Fowlerville, Michigan, Gehringer signed with the Detroit Tigers before he was 21, played a few games for them in 1924 and 1925, performed in 2 minor-league towns and then put in the rest of his career with Detroit.

There was no flamboyance in Gehringer either on or off the field. Even during his active days fans were often surprised to be reminded that he was the best second baseman in the league, for it was Gehringer's habit to stay out of the spotlight and to do nothing to earn himself extra notice in the newspapers.

Gehringer had his first great year at bat in 1934, when the Tigers won their first pennant in 25 years. Charley hit .356 that season. But three seasons later he made it .371 and led the American League. He was named the Most Valuable Player in the league that year. In his 19 seasons with Detroit, he hit for less than .300 only five times (in his first season, 1924, when he played in only 5 games, he batted .545). In 3 successive All-Star Games, he had exactly the same batting average: .667. In the fourth he hit .600.

# HENRY BENJAMIN GREENBERG was hitting
home runs for Detroit when Babe Ruth was still hitting them for the Yankees and one year big Hank nearly tied Babe's record. He hit 58 homers in 1938.

No right-handed batter ever hit more home runs in a season than Hank Greenberg did. (Jimmy Foxx hit just as many.) With Detroit he hit better than .300 in every full season he

Greenberg, right, receiving
Most Valuable Player
award from Judge Landis, 1936.

Gehringer (scoring) used
to "take" the first pitch, he said,
"so the pitcher could start even."

played, except the last one, 1946, when he hit only .277. (In 1941, when he interrupted his baseball career to enter the service, he played but 19 games.) And in that final full season, despite the falling off of his average, he still contrived to knock 44 fair balls out of the park, leading the league for the fourth time (with one tie).

Hank Greenberg was not the fanciest-fielding of first basemen. In two seasons he led the league in errors. But he also managed to lead the league three times in putouts and twice in assists. He was a quiet, determined, workmanlike player who was always putting out his best for the team. He once played out a ball game with two bones broken in his wrist. He played the outfield toward the end of his career in Detroit but when he was sold to Pittsburgh in 1947 he went back to playing first base—and hit 25 home runs.

When he had become too old to play, Hank moved to the business end of baseball and, teamed with Bill Veeck, had a hand in bringing pennants first to Cleveland and then to Chicago.

# ROBERT MOSES GROVE called Lefty, was one of the fastest pitchers who ever lived; when he started playing ball for money, in Midland, Maryland, he played first base, because there was not a catcher in the area who could hold his fiery fast ball. When a boy was found who could hold Grove's pitches, Bob gained fame quickly and graduated from Midland to Martinsburg, West Virginia, and then to the Baltimore Orioles. With the Orioles he became the best pitcher in the International League and he was sold to the Philadelphia Athletics for $100,600. (The extra $600 was added to the check to make the price a record. Babe Ruth had been sold to the Yankees for $100,000.)

It took Lefty Grove 2 seasons to become a successful big-league pitcher, for he was careless at first of his control. But once having won 20 games in 1927 (appearing in 51 games), he went 6 more seasons without winning less than 20. For 3 straight seasons Lefty led the American League in both earned-run average and won-lost percentage. And after he injured his arm and was sold to the Boston Red Sox (for more than that $100,600) he developed a fine curve and "fork-ball" change of pace that gave him 6 more winning and 2 break-even seasons until he had finally attained his goal of 300 victories.

# CHARLES LEO HARTNETT was one of the most talkative and most aggressive men who ever played major league baseball—and one of the best liked. He caught on quickly with the Chicago Cubs (after a season in Worcester, in the Eastern League), because the Cub pitching star, Grover Cleveland Alexander, took a liking to him and insisted that he be his catcher. Before long the fans and the players all shared Alexander's preference, for Gabby had a way with him. He would strut to his position like a man about to announce his claim to ownership of the ball park, greet opponents and fans with an all-inclusive wave of his big hand, and then drive his clenched fist into the air to indicate that the battle was on.

Gabby always played with every ounce of his strength. Despite his size (he was one of the heartiest eaters in baseball), he never loafed, never looked for the easy way, never failed to try for that extra advantage.

He was sure-handed, cool, and confidence-inspiring. In all his career with the Cubs he dropped but 3 high fouls behind the plate. He seldom caught fewer than 100 games for the Cubs. But when he had to lay aside his catching gear one year because of a sore arm, he was kept on as a pinch-hitter and drove in 9 runs in 22 times at bat. In 1937, he hit .354 in 110 games, the high mark of his career. In 1930, he hit 37 home runs.

Gabby was appointed to manage the Cubs in 1938, when there were 25 games left to play and the Cubs were 6½ games off the pace. With Gabby in the lead, the Cubs captured 21 victories and took the pennant. Gabby himself won the decisive game by driving out a home run in a game with Pittsburgh, with the score tied, 2 men out, and 2 strikes on him.

# ROGERS HORNSBY is generally regarded as the greatest right-handed batter who ever played big-league ball. His unique batting stance—feet together, standing as far back and as far away from the plate as the batter's box would allow—has seldom been imitated with any real success. In the era of the

Lefty Grove, who pitched for both the Red Sox and Athletics, won 300 games in 17 seasons.

With the A's, Lefty was a fireballer. With the Red Sox, he turned "cute" and lasted until he was 41.

Charles Hartnett, Cubs'
catcher, was called "Gabby"
because of his chatter.
He kept fans and teammates
stirred to fever heat.

Gabby managed the Chicago
Cubs for three seasons (1938-40)
and played first base for a
time. In 1937 he batted .354.

Rogers Hornsby, called the
game's greatest right-handed batter,
stood as far from the plate as
the batting box allowed.
He batted .424 in 1924.

Above, Hornsby hits a homer
in a practice game in Los Angeles
after the Cubs bought him from
Boston for $250,000.

lively ball no one ever hit more often than Hornsby did. From 1921 to 1925, he never hit for an average of less than .384 and he three times hit over .400. In 1924, he attained the "modern" batting record of .424.

Hornsby was a great fielder too, with a quick and accurate "double-play" throw, made right across his chest without shifting his feet—the most difficult throw for a second baseman to make. Indeed it was his fielding (when he was a shortstop in Denison, Texas) that first attracted the attention of big-league scouts. When he came up to the St. Louis Cardinals in 1915, he choked his bat and hit from a crouch, bending close to the plate as the ball came in. It was not until he had adopted his far-back, free-swinging style that he began to attain high batting marks. With the Cardinals, he played shortstop, first base, and third base before he even tried out at second, where he was to become the top performer of his day.

In his first full season at St. Louis, after he had learned to change his batting posture, and began to hit to all fields, shifting with the pitch, he made a mark of .313. For his remaining time in the big leagues he had only three seasons under .300 and he had just as many full seasons over .400. He won the National League batting championship six times in a row, and seven times altogether.

# CARL OWEN HUBBELL is the only major league player of the post-1900 era to earn the old-fashioned nickname of "King." He also became known to sports writers as the "Meal Ticket" because of his reliability: in his 16 years with the New York Giants, the only major league team he ever pitched for, Hubbell had only 1 losing season. That was in 1940, when he won 11 and lost 12.

Hubbell, a tall, skinny left-hander with beetling eyebrows, was a deliberate worker on the mound. His favorite weapon was his "screwball" pitch—a reverse curve thrown by turning the thumb in rather than out on delivery, so that when thrown by a left-hander the ball breaks in toward a left-handed hitter.

Hubbell pitched a no-hit game against Pittsburgh in 1929 and pitched an 18-inning shutout against St. Louis in 1933 in which he did not issue a base on balls. In 1936, after his arm had gone bad and he had an operation to remedy it, he threw 16 victories in a row, and 8 more to begin the next year. In 1933, he pitched 46⅓ consecutive shutout innings for a National League record. He had 10 shutouts that year.

His best-remembered feat, however, is his striking out the pride of the American League in the 1934 All-Star Game. Babe Ruth, Lou Gehrig, Jimmy Foxx, Al Simmons, and Joe Cronin all went down on strikes before the screwball wizard. It took only 6 screwballs to dispose of Ruth and Gehrig.

# KENESAW MOUNTAIN LANDIS is credited with

having saved organized baseball from collapse after the Black Sox scandals of 1919. Judge Landis was made First Commissioner of Baseball and set about purging the game of the men who were undertaking to corrupt it. He ruled a number of players out of baseball for life and even disciplined those who played with such men on teams outside his jurisdiction. The result was that, within a year or two, organized baseball's face had been thoroughly scrubbed and the whole tone of the game — both as a business and as a spectacle — was improved.

Judge Landis also made a point of seeing that the spectators received fair treatment. Once he ordered the entire proceeds of a World Series game donated to charity because the fans felt that the game had been called off, when the score was tied, without good reason. He made it his business to investigate the fairness of player contracts and to prevent, when he could, the unfair "hiding" of players in the minor leagues until the parent club was ready for them. By declaring such men free agents, Landis broke up a system that had sometimes resulted in denying a talented player a chance to sell his services for the best price.

Before becoming Commissioner of Baseball, Judge Landis, as a Federal District Judge, had heard the suit brought by the "outlaw" Federal League in 1915 against the National and American Leagues, who, the Federal League charged, were conspiring to limit competition. Landis, in order to see the matter settled peaceably, postponed any decision until the

Giants' Carl Hubbell
on May 4th, 1937 (below),
pitched his 19th win
in a row, over two seasons.

Hubbell's best pitch
was his screwball or reverse
curve, which never came
when the batter expected it.

Kenesaw Mountain Landis,
a small but commanding figure,
liked dramatic poses. He
never wore his hat for pictures.

Landis was death on the
"farm" system, but in spite of him
baseball club owners built
extensive holdings.

The only time Joe McCarthy wore a major-league uniform was when he led Cubs, Yankees, and Red Sox.

McCarthy won one pennant with the Cubs and eight with the New York Yankees.

older leagues had bought out the interests of the Federal League club owners. It was his circumspect handling of this matter that prompted the club owners to turn to him in 1920, when the Black Sox scandal seemed to be destroying public confidence in the game's honesty.

## JOSEPH VINCENT McCARTHY until he was
made manager of the Chicago National League Club in 1926, had never even set foot inside a big-league dugout. Joe played second base, third base, shortstop, and outfield in the American Association and that was as close as he ever came. He first made his reputation as manager of Louisville, in the American Association, where he won 1 pennant and finished in the first division six times out of seven tries.

Joe became one of the greatest of managers because he knew how to take charge. He did not bully his men, as managers of the old school liked to do, nor was he one of the boys, as a few of his own predecessors had been. He could hold a loose rein on men like Grover Cleveland Alexander or Babe Ruth or Hack Wilson and be tough as a prison guard with some fresh kid who did not feel like trying. He had firm faith in his own judgment of players and let no question of sentiment or public pressure sway him when he thought it was time to let a man go. In Chicago, he turned the Cubs from a second-division team to a pennant winner in 4 seasons. 2 years later he came to New York, and within 2 more years brought his Yankees in first to beat the Cubs out of a World Championship.

With the New York Yankees McCarthy established a team reputation for "class"—which included dignity on the field and off, a minimum of argument with umpires, strict decorum and neat dress in public, and winning baseball at the Yankee Stadium. Under Joe McCarthy, the New York Yankees won 8 pennants and 7 World Championships.

## WILLIAM BOYD McKECHNIE a switch-hitting
infielder, was called "Deacon" because he looked and acted like one. A soft-spoken, religious man, who avoided strong drink, Bill was still tough-fibered enough to hold a rein on the

Deacon Bill McKechnie won pennants in three major league cities but ended his career as a coach.

most rambunctious player. It was his skill at managing that won him a place in the Hall of Fame, for his actual play was no more than average. He is the only manager who ever won pennants in three different major league cities.

Only once in his life did Bill hit over .300. That was in 1914 when he was playing third base for Indianapolis in the Federal League, where Edd Roush was also playing. He and Roush moved together to Newark, where Bill became manager; and they went to the Giants together and then were traded at the same time to the Reds. By this time most of McKechnie's major league career was behind him. After starting in the Pennsylvania-Ohio-Maryland League, Bill had signed with Pittsburgh in 1907 and played but three games (at third base and second base) before being sent down to Canton of the Ohio-Pennsylvania League. In 1911, he was back with Pittsburgh for two and a half seasons, put in part of two seasons with St. Paul in the American Association, went to the Boston Braves as an outfielder and was quickly waived to the New York Yankees, where manager Frank Chance kept him on despite his feeble work at the bat. "He has brains," Chance explained.

Bill had six more seasons in the majors as a player. In July 1922, he was made manager of the Pirates when the team was in sixth place, finished the season in fourth place and won the pennant three seasons later. In 1927 he joined St. Louis as a coach and in 1928 he was made manager and won the pennant. He was sent to Rochester that same year because he failed to win a single game in the World Series. He had his Rochester team in first place when the Cardinals called him back. The next year he moved to Boston and, after eight lean years with the Boston Braves, he returned to Cincinnati and won two pennants in a row, 1939 and 1940. In 1946, he ended his managerial career and signed as a coach with the Cleveland Indians. He went with Lou Boudreau to Boston, for two seasons, before retiring, at the age of 66, after 48 years in the game.

# MELVIN THOMAS OTT never played minor league ball in his life, and spent his playing career with one club.

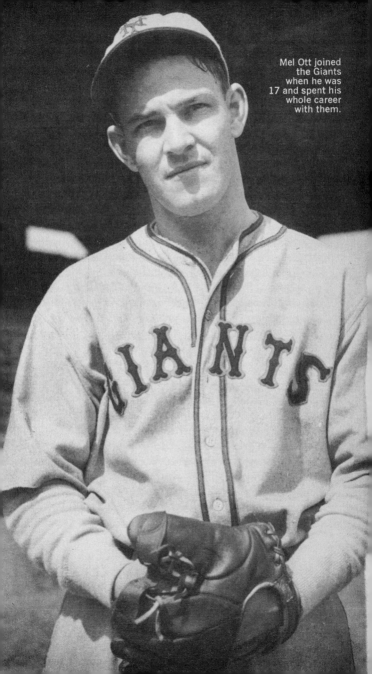

Mel Ott joined the Giants when he was 17 and spent his whole career with them.

John McGraw of the Giants turned Ott into an outfielder, helped teach him how to run, and let him concentrate on his strong, level batting swing. Ott's peculiar stance at the plate was entirely his own. He stood with feet far apart, and stepped forward only a few inches as he swung. But he made that step by lifting his front foot (the right foot) high in the air and bringing it sharply down just before he met the ball. This motion, he said, gave him extra leverage. It did indeed result in many home runs, for Ott "pulled" every pitch, and the short right-field fence in the Polo Grounds seemed made to order for him.

Ott set National League all-time records in home runs (511), runs scored (1859), and runs batted in (1860). He also set the league mark for bases on balls (1708). In 8 seasons he hit 30 or more home runs and one year (1929) he hit 42. He was a first-rate outfielder too, despite the heavily muscled legs that helped power his bat but kept him from being a speedster in the field. His mighty arm, and his skill at playing caroms off the short Polo Grounds fences, made him into a menace to opposing runners. One year (1935) he led all right fielders in the league in fielding percentage. He was manager of the Giants from 1942 to 1948.

# HERBERT JEFFERIS PENNOCK the great left-handed pitcher (and switch batter), is another player who spent all his adult life in organized baseball. He pitched in the American League for 22 seasons, with Philadelphia, Boston, and New York, then became a coach with the Boston Red Sox, then supervisor of their farm system, and finally general manager of the Philadelphia Phillies. In between, he had played in the International League, with Providence for part of 1915 and with Buffalo for part of the following season.

A control pitcher chiefly, who would not throw 10 fast balls in a game, Pennock pitched $7\frac{1}{3}$ perfect innings in the World Series of 1923 for the Yankees against the Pittsburgh Pirates and he never lost a World Series game (he won 5). In his 10 World Series appearances, Pennock gave up only 8 walks. He pitched both sidearm and overhand and could make a ball curve both ways. His change of pace was as good as any in the

Herb Pennock won five
World Series games
and never lost one. He
pitched 22 seasons.

league in his day, so his lack of a fast ball did not deter him.

When he was 40 years old, Pennock brought his active career to a close but in that final year (1934) Herb worked in 30 games as relief pitcher for the Red Sox and posted an earned-run average of 3.05.

# EDGAR CHARLES (SAM) RICE of the Washington Senators hit 182 singles in 1925, to establish an American League record, and he got a share of another record when he went to bat 600 times or more in 8 seasons. Except for these feats, however, Sam made few appearances in the record books. Yet he hit the ball solidly and consistently for 18 seasons with the Senators, and he was ranked among the game's top outfielders for more than a decade. He was fast, sharp-eyed, deadly on fly balls, and he owned a rifle arm.

Sam started out as a pitcher, like most strong-armed youths. But he could not establish himself on the mound. He had 1 winning season (9—2) with Petersburg in the Virginia League, and 1 losing season (11—12), in which he struck out 153 batters. With Washington he pitched 1 game at the end of his career and won that. When he joined the Senators in July 1915 he found a team that was loaded with pitchers—led by the best of them all, Walter Johnson.

By the middle of the next season Sam (so christened by a sportswriter who couldn't remember his real name) was trying to argue himself into the line-up. Finally Manager Clark Griffith, having already used Walter Johnson as a pinch-hitter and part-time outfielder, let Sam pinch-hit. (In 1915 he had hit 3 home runs in 8 times at bat.) Sam immediately displayed his value at the plate and got himself a full-time job as an outfieder. In his first game as a regular, Rice hit a double, a triple, and a single, fired several balls in on a trolley wire from right field, and covered his area as if he had been raised there. In the final 13 games of the 1916 season, he got 20 hits in 54 times at bat. The next year he displayed a new talent— blazing speed on the basepaths—and before he grew old he had earned the nick-name "Man o' War."

In Sam's 19 full seasons with Washington, his batting average dropped under .300 only 4 times. In 1916 he hit .299; in

Sam Rice
was called Sam
because a writer
forgot his
real name
was Edgar.

Jackie Robinson (left)
batted .342 for the
Dodgers in 1949.

(Above) Jackie Robinson revived
the art of stealing home.

1922 he hit .295; in 1927, .297; in 1933, .294. In 1934 he was sold to the Cleveland Indians and hit .293 in 97 games.

What most people recall about Sam Rice is his tremendous skill in the field. And perhaps the greatest feat of his life—and possibly the greatest play ever made at the Washington ball park—was Sam's leaping catch of a sure home run that big Earl Smith of Pittsburgh popped into the centerfield stands in the 1925 World Series. Sam had been moved to center for this Series, to make room for another slugger. When the Smith blow came his way, he timed it perfectly, leaped high into the air, nailed the ball and sailed right over the low fence into the laps of the bleacher bugs. One of the fans snatched the ball away from Sam, but the umpire ruled it a fair catch and the fans screamed in delight and disbelief for over a minute. Sam wrestled the ball away from the fan and held it up in the air as he climbed back into the park.

**JACK ROOSEVELT ROBINSON** the first Negro to enter organized ball, was also one of the greatest infielders ever to play the game. A fiery competitor and a dedicated team-player, he inspired his teammates and demoralized the opposition. Robinson set no great records as a hitter, a base-runner, or a fielder. But no man since Ty Cobb's day could stir such excitement by his very presence on the basepaths. Always alert, and always on the move, he unsettled many a pitcher by his daring fakes and blazing take-offs. He brought back into baseball one of its most thrilling features, the head-long steal of home. Robinson was a solid and authoritative hitter. In his best year (1949) he batted .342. But there was no percentage in a pitcher's walking him to get at a weaker batter, for Robinson, once he stood on base, threatened to come all the way around.

Robinson reached big league baseball rather late in life, via the Kansas City Monarchs of the Negro league, and Montreal of the International League. One of the most popular men ever to play for Montreal, Robinson was almost 30 years old when he finally graduated to the Brooklyn Dodgers in 1947. With Brooklyn he played every infield position, as well as the outfield. His very presence in the line-up seemed enough to raise the team to new heights of accomplishment, for he was ready to extend himself at any time to win the game and he transferred his own enthusiasm to his team-mates. At bat, he was ready to bunt, to play hit-and-run, to swing for the fences, or even to get hit with the ball (he was hit seven times in one season). His being a Negro naturally attracted more attention to his performance in that day. But he was an extraordinary ballplayer by any lights and earned his position by his inspired, and inspiring, play.

Robinson led the league in stolen bases with 29 in 1947, his first year in the majors. In 1948 he was the top second-baseman in the league on defense. But even when he was not outstripping all others, he was a constant menace to the other side. No one who ever saw him play—rangy, loose-limbed, reckless and determined—will ever forget him.

# EDD J. ROUSH the pride of Indiana, was christened with the two D's in his name. Roush (pronounced Rowsh) is one of the few members of the Hall of Fame who played in three major leagues: The outlaw Federal as well as the American and National. Edd is remembered, wherever he played, for his spectacular defensive play and many fans will hold that he is the best outfielder who ever lived. He made an intense study of batters, so he could position himself properly when they came to bat. But his lightning speed enabled him to reach almost anything hit into center field. In Indianapolis, in Newark, in New York, and in Cincinnati he left memories of over-the-shoulder catches, charging shoe-string grabs, and leaping one-handed saves.

His hitting too was steady and strong, despite his habit of moving about in the box and trying to outguess the pitchers. Apparently he often guessed right, for he led the National League in his second season there (1917) with an average of .341 and led it again in 1919 with an average of .321.

Edd's major league career began with the Chicago White Sox, in 1914, after two seasons in the minors. It was in the Federal League, however, that he came into his own. He starred in center field at Indianapolis and Newark, and when the league collapsed he was picked up, along with Manager

Edd Roush played in
three major leagues
and made great catches in
all of them.

Bill McKechnie, by the New York Giants. They quickly traded him to Cincinnati and he stayed there for ten seasons. He returned then to the Giants for 3 seasons and, after he had stayed home for a whole year rather than accept a salary he thought inadequate, he was allowed to sign again with the Reds and finished his active career with them in 1931.

Roush had been noted as a hold-out even before he stayed home for a season. But it was not always salary that prompted him. He was an abstemious man, always in good condition, and he felt that long spring training wasted both his time and money. No matter how late he reported, it never took him more than a few days to get into playing shape.

# GEORGE HERMAN RUTH hit so many home runs
in his major league career (714) that some fans forget that he could do everything well on a baseball diamond. He had a fine throwing arm, made many a circus catch in the outfield, ran the bases with skill, speed, and determination, and was one of the best sliders in the business. And first of all he was a left-handed pitcher, one of the finest who ever pitched for the Boston Red Sox. In 1916, he led the American League pitchers with an earned-run average of 1.75. He pitched 3 World Series games—1 in 1916 and 2 in 1918—and won them all. He set the all-time record at the same time for pitching consecutive scoreless World Series innings (29⅔), a record which stood until 1961. At first base, he was deft as a dancer; and when he first played baseball—at an industrial school for wayward boys—he was the catcher, and not even a right-handed glove that he had to remove before he could throw kept him from being the best in his small circuit.

But of course it was as a hitter that Ruth earned his greatest fame and made his deepest impression on the game. Almost alone he awoke the baseball world to the box-office value of the home run. He not only caused the Yankee Stadium to be built, he caused many a ball club to redesign its park to make home runs more frequent. He changed batting styles from the sandlots to the majors, as every man who came to the plate began to swing the full length of the bat and to try to put every pitch over the fence. He also prompted the

Baseball never saw
a man to equal Babe Ruth
as a personality and
as a player.

Above, Babe Ruth,
standing, left, poses at
contract signing with Red Sox
brass: Owner Harry Frazee,
seated, right;
Secretary Ed Barrow, left.

Ruth hits his first of two homers
against Philadelphia, April 12, 1932,
to open his 19th season. Gehrig
also hit two in this game.

At the close of his career,
Babe often played first base.
He had been a great
pitcher, too.

Babe Ruth, wearing his famous
number 3 for the last time,
accepts Stadium ovation
two months before his death.

doctoring of the ball, to increase its "jack-rabbit" quality, that has caused spasmodic controversy ever since.

Babe Ruth, who was always called "Jidge" by his playmates (Jidge is the New England diminutive for George), was surely the most famous player the professional game ever knew. His name and face were recognized around the world by men and women who would not have understood a box score or known how to hold a bat. Long after he had left the game, he was still a box-office attraction and today his name lives on in the Babe Ruth leagues, where boys in cities throughout the land learn to play organized baseball.

Whether Ty Cobb and Honus Wagner were greater players than Ruth no one can really say. Ruth played his type of baseball better than any other man who ever lived. And there is no denying that his fame, his influence, even his salaries and his dissipations, outstripped those of all other baseball players before or since.

When Ruth entered baseball, right out of the industrial school, he became a pitcher for the Baltimore Orioles in the International League. A skinny, moon-faced boy with a very large head and long legs, he looked little like the gargantuan figure that eventually would win recognition at every way station in the world. In his first spring at Baltimore, in 1914, Ruth pitched an exhibition game against the World Champion Athletics and beat them, and he opened his professional career soon afterward by pitching a shutout against Buffalo. He never hit a single home run for Baltimore (except in exhibition games). He was, instead, one of the fastest left-handed pitchers in the league. In July he was purchased by the Boston Red Sox and farmed to Providence, in the same league as Baltimore. With Providence, where he occasionally played first base, Babe hit his only minor league home run. He won 22 games in the International League that year, and also won 2 games in the American League for the Red Sox. Next year, he was top pitcher on the Red Sox staff. He continued to pitch regularly all the time he was with Boston, although he more and more frequently moved to the outfield until by 1919, when he broke the home-run record with 29 four-baggers in a season, he pitched in only 17 of the 130 games he played. In 1920, he was sold to the Yankees for $100,000, and from that time forth he was the game's greatest hitter. He set a new home-run record immediately, by getting 54 in 142 games. Next year he broke the record again, with 59, and 6 years later, at the age of 32, he set the all-time record of 60 in 154 games. He wound up his career in 1935 with the Boston Braves, after refusing to play again for the Yankees unless he was made manager. Playing first base for the Braves, and serving as assistant manager, Babe faded badly at the plate. He got into only 28 games and hit only 6 home runs. But 3 of them came on the same day, in Forbes Field, Pittsburgh, in a game against the Pirates. And his last one—the last he would ever hit—was, some fans recall, the longest ball ever hit at that park.

# ALOYSIUS HARRY SIMMONS (Szymanski) was

known throughout the baseball world in his day as the man who hit with one foot "in the bucket"—that is, with his forward foot striding toward third base rather than toward the pitcher. This stance was supposed to keep a man from ever becoming a good hitter. But it had no such effect on Al.

Raised in Milwaukee, Al wanted to become a professional ballplayer from the time he could understand the game. He led the American League in batting only twice, in 1930 and 1931, with averages of .381 and .390. But he was always among the leaders and earned a major league average of .334, with a high mark of .392 in 1927, when Harry Heilmann led the league with an average of .398.

Al could hit the ball far as well as frequently. On July 15, 1932, he hit 3 home runs in one game. In the fourth game of the 1929 World Series he went to bat twice in the seventh inning, opening it with a home run and then hitting a single when he appeared again, scoring the first and the ninth run in this 10-run inning. But he had done something like that once before: on June 15, 1925, in a game against Cleveland, he hit a single the first time up in the eighth inning and hit a home run when he came to the plate again in the same inning.

Al Simmons (left), was called
"Foot-in-the-bucket," but
he really kept front foot free
to hit to any field.

George Sisler (above), deemed
the most graceful fielder
in the game, started out as a
pitcher and became a
topnotch batter.

He began and ended his career with the Philadelphia Athletics, having played 20 seasons in both major leagues.

# GEORGE HAROLD SISLER a left-hander, had a

natural advantage at first base and at the plate. He led American League first basemen in assists 6 times—and once led the National League too.

Only Ty Cobb ever earned as high a season's batting average in the American League as George Sisler did when he hit .420 in 1922. (Cobb made his mark 11 years earlier.) In 1920, Sisler had posted a league-leading mark of .407 and that year he established the all-time major league record for total hits in a season: 257.

Sisler was a graceful performer at the plate and in the infield, where he played first base for the St. Louis Browns and the Boston Braves (with a few games for the Washington Senators). He was swift on the basepaths and owned a strong and cunning arm.

He started out in baseball as a college pitcher. In his first year with St. Louis, Sisler won 4 out of 9 games as a pitcher and batted .285. The next year he stopped pitching and hit .305, and never again in his major league career (which was interrupted for a full season by eye trouble) did he drop below that figure for a season's work.

Sisler was a batter in the tradition of Willie Keeler—ready to hit to all fields, to bunt if he found the infield playing deep, or to use a "Baltimore chop" if they tried to anticipate a bunt. He was extremely fast, and batting left-handed as he did, he was able to turn many a bunt into a base hit. But he could hit the ball hard too and one year (1920), just after Babe Ruth had broken all records with his amazing (for that day) total of 29 home runs, Sisler collected 19.

# WILLIAM HAROLD TERRY who was born in

Atlanta, Georgia, was a New York Giant for his entire major league career. Bill was a scientific hitter. He batted left-handed and was ready to hit to any field. He took a business-like attitude toward baseball, and he studied the job of hitting. In his 12 full seasons with the Giants he fell below .300 only once, in 1926, when he was on the bench a good part of the time. In 1930, he hit .401, and in more than 30 years no other National Leaguer has reached that magic mark.

Bill's cold-bloodedness was notorious, thanks to the sports writers who found him difficult to deal with. He was not interested in being "popular" or "colorful." He seldom showed any excitement or strain. He just performed his job in a tenacious, determined way, never slacking, never loafing, never showing off.

Terry began to play ball in Texas, as a pitcher and out-fielder. But he was too good a hitter to stay out of the line-up and when McGraw found him in Memphis he determined to make the young man a first baseman. After Terry signed with the Giants he was farmed out to Toledo, where he made an intensive study of his new first-base job. When he came up to the Giants he seemed like a veteran in the position.

When McGraw stepped down as manager in 1932, it was Bill Terry who took over, delighting McGraw with his crafty strategy in the 1933 World Series, after Terry had won his first pennant. But Terry never won another World Series, although he put his team into 2 more. His strategy never really compensated for the lack of his own heavy bat or for the lack of inspiration his own dogged play provided.

# HAROLD JOSEPH TRAYNOR called Pie, was raised in Somerville, Massachusetts, where he was a school hero in football and baseball. He wanted most of all to play baseball for the Boston Braves. The Braves had a scout who lived near young Traynor and the scout urged him to go to Braves Field and work out. But when Traynor got there, the Braves manager, George Stallings, ran him out of the place without even giving him a trial and told him not to come back. This was in 1918, when Pie was 18 years old. Unfortunately for the Braves, Pie Traynor did come back 2 years later, as third baseman for the Pittsburgh Pirates, and kept on coming back (except for 1 year in Birmingham) every year of the next 17.

In Pittsburgh he became the best third baseman of his day, a man whom John McGraw called "the greatest team player

Bill Terry (left), made a
business of baseball.
But he always wanted to win.

Pie Traynor (above), one
of the biggest third basemen,
was a speedster too.

in baseball." Traynor was an even-tempered, self-effacing man who was put out of a ball game only once in his career. But he was a demon competitor who could do everything well. Big for a third baseman (6 feet 1), he was rangy and fast and owned the strongest arm of his era. He could steal ground balls from the shortstop, spear line drives at the baseline, pluck fouls out of the stand, scoop bunts on the run and rifle the ball to first.

Traynor could wallop the ball too. He hit .366 for Pittsburgh in 1930 and had 9 other seasons when he hit over .300. In 1923, when he hit .338, he made 12 home runs and tied for the league leadership in three-baggers (19). In that same year he also topped all third basemen in putouts and assists.

Traynor became manager of the Pirates in 1934, managed from the bench in 1936, came back to play 5 games in 1937, and retired from baseball in 1939, when he was almost 40.

# ARTHUR CHARLES VANCE was 29 years old by the time he made the grade in the major leagues. He had failed in three previous attempts to catch on. Finally, Dazzy (he called himself "the Dazzler," but the name, like so many baseball nicknames, was a babyhood pet name) posted 18 wins for Brooklyn in 1922 and led the league with 134 strikeouts. He led the league for the next 6 seasons in that department, attaining a high mark of 262 in 1924, when he was voted the Most Valuable Player in the league.

Vance's irreverent attitude and his easy sense of humor, along with his tremendous speed and willingness to use it, made him a great favorite in Brooklyn, where he fit in with the eccentric crew that earned themselves a dozen different nicknames to indicate that they were all a little touched in the head. Vance organized the "0 for 4" club, of teammates who achieved a perfect zero in 4 trips to the plate.

But on the pitching mound, with his loose underwear shirt flapping, his red face pouring sweat, and his tremendous bulk thrown behind every pitch, Vance was no joke to the opposition. He won 28 games for Brooklyn in 1924 and 22 in 1925, the season in which he pitched his only no-hitter, against Philadelphia on September 13. In his big year, 1924, he once

Dazzy Vance was almost 30 by the time he reached the big leagues.

struck out 7 men in a row. In a 10-inning game against St. Louis in 1925, Vance struck out 17 batters.

# PAUL GLEE WANER a short, wiry young man when he started in baseball, was but 5 feet 8 inches tall and weighed a little more than 150 pounds all his career. At the bat, however, he was too big for most pitchers and they named him Big Poison. (Little Poison was his brother Lloyd, younger and even smaller.)

His merry middle name and the fact that he was born in a place named "Harrah" (Oklahoma) were well suited to Paul Waner's nature. He enjoyed life and he enjoyed baseball and was a popular companion. He liked late hours and good times but better still he liked to help his team win ball games. Paul was a team player who was concerned not so much with his average as with his getting the hit the team needed in a pinch. He had a habit of fouling off good pitches, when a hit was not vital, so that a pitcher might be misled into feeding him that same pitch when there were men on base who had to be brought in. A remarkably sharp-eyed man, he might have posted batting averages as high as any ever registered had he not been so concerned with winning ball games.

Still, Paul did lead the National League 3 times during his 15 seasons with the Pittsburgh Pirates. In his first year with the Pirates he led the league in triples—the speedboys' specialty—and the next year he led in hits, triples, runs batted in, and in batting average.

He ended his career finally in 1946, with Miami, Florida, where he batted .325 in 62 games. But before he quit the majors, while he was still with the Boston Braves in 1942, Waner got the hit he wanted most—his 3000th in the big leagues, to become the only modern National Leaguer, besides Honus Wagner, to achieve that mark. (Stan Musial has now also joined this distinguished group.)

Paul Waner, called "Big Poison," gets his 3000th hit with Braves.

# LATE ARRIVALS

HERE ARE A FEW MEMBERS ELECTED SINCE 1966.

Ross Young was a little fellow,
like John McGraw, and like McGraw he
was full of fight. When he died at
the age of thirty, he had just attained
his peak with the Giants.

**JACOB PETER BECKLEY** was the greatest baseball name in Pittsburgh before anyone had ever heard of Honus Wagner. Jake, known as "Eagle-Eye" for his ability to pick all sorts of pitches out of the air and drive them to and often over the distant fences, was the slugging first baseman of the club that was not yet called the Pirates. These were the days when first basemen were all built like boilermakers, when slugging was all that was required, and skill afield was of no account at that position as long as the man could catch the throws. Jake was no match in size for monsters like Dan Brouthers and Roger Connor, but he was solidly built all the same—just a few pounds lighter than Brouthers, while four inches shorter. Jake could run fast, too, and he was a pretty good fielder (he leads all first basemen in total chances and putouts). But he had a hopelessly weak arm, the weakest in the league. Hitting was his specialty and he loved it. And how he wanted to win!

One day, playing for Cincinnati against his old Pittsburgh teammates, when he made a poor toss to the pitcher at first, allowing a runner to get all the way to third, Jake saw that the man was going to try to score. Knowing that he could never throw the ball to the catcher, Jake started on a dead run for the plate. The runner, Tommy Leach, started his slide for home and Jake leaped for him. He landed on top of Tommy, put him out, and broke three of Tommy's ribs. Efforts like this, along with his mighty hitting, won Jake his big following in Pittsburgh and, later, in Cincinnati.

Jake, born in Hannibal, Missouri, started to play ball for money with the Leavenworth, Kansas, team when he was 18 years old, in 1886. Next year he played all summer with the Lincoln, Nebraska, ball club and played all winter for the fast club in Stockton, California. That gave Jake 3 full seasons of experience in 2 years.

At the start of the 1888 season, he came back home to play for the St. Louis Whites (there were also Browns and Reds in that city). But he was promptly spotted by the

Pittsburgh management and he started with Pittsburgh in June. Except for 1 season with the Pittsburgh club in the Players League, Beckley stayed with the Pittsburgh Nationals for most of 8 seasons.

In 1896, the New York Giants, trying to build themselves into a winner, paid Pittsburgh a fat price for Jake's contract and he came to New York to take over first base from "Dirty Jack" Doyle, one of the roughest players in the league. Jake's hitting fell off a little in New York. He had been hitting .328 in Pittsburgh, but with New York his average dropped to .302. And in 1897, when he was sharing the first-base job with Wee Willie Walker, he hit only .250 in the first 17 games. In June, the impatient Giant management sold him to Cincinnati and he began at once to slug the ball in his familiar style. In the balance of the season with the Reds, he hit .345.

Jake's most enjoyable day in baseball, however, came when he returned to St. Louis to hit three home runs in one game before the hometown folks. He stayed with Cincinnati until 1904 when he was traded to the St. Louis Cardinals. By this time, Jake was one of only three major-league players who still wore the old-time handlebar mustaches. (The others were Monte Cross of the Athletics and Silent John Titus of the Phillies.)

With the Cardinals, his batting gradually fell off and in 1907, he played his last game of major-league ball, rounding out 20 full seasons as an active major-league player. He was hired at once to manage the Kansas City club in the American Association, but hung on there only 2 seasons, when he was released. In 1911, he signed to play with the bush-league club in Topeka. After all, he was **only** 43.

# LAWRENCE PETER BERRA became Yogi while he was still in school, from some supposed resemblance to a Yoga practitioner. He grew up, as many great ballplayers have, in St. Louis and first played ball on the playgrounds

Jake Beckley had the worst throwing
arm in the major leagues in his day—
and the sharpest batting eye.

Yogi Berra might have become a
Cardinal rather than a Yankee, if the
St. Louis club had been willing to
come up with an extra $200.

there. George Weiss of the Yankees heard about him from a St. Louis tavern-keeper for whom George had once secured World Series tickets. By the time the Yankee scout came to look at Berra, the young man had been scouted and rejected by the St. Louis ball club, which had signed his pal, Joe Garagiola, for a $500 bonus. They offered Larry $300. But Larry said he wanted "just what Joey got" and the club decided he was not worth it.

But George Weiss thought Berra was a bargain at the price, and signed him immediately. Whereupon Larry went to play for the Yankee farm club in Norfolk, in the Piedmont League. He caught 11 games there in 1943 and earned promotion to the Kansas City club, even though he batted only .253, with 7 home runs. That was a respectable average for a catcher—but not for Berra. He was out to wallop the ball harder than that, for hitting was his chief desire.

Yogi never did play for Kansas City, however, for the navy took him away in 1944 and 1945, and he soon had men on both sides of the Atlantic talking about his powerful hitting with his service nine. A few club owners made efforts to sign him and were jolted to learn that he had already been "discovered" by George Weiss, who would not let him go for any price. Indeed, when Berra came back from the war to play for the top Yankee farm club in Newark, Weiss used to hustle out of his office whenever Yogi came to bat, so he could stand and admire Yogi's mighty swing.

At Newark, where he caught and played the outfield for part of the season of 1946, Yogi hit 15 home runs and batted .314. He was moved right up to the Yankees before the season ended and hit 2 home runs in 22 times at bat.

The Yankees tried Berra as both outfielder and catcher. He had much to learn about both jobs, so they settled finally for making him into a catcher. Had he been less of a hitter, they'd have abandoned the task, for Berra, in his first few seasons, was almost a liability behind the plate. In the 1947 World Series with the Dodgers, however, Berra demonstrated his real value by hitting a pinch-hit home run in the third game, becoming the first pinch-hitter in World Series history ever to perform that feat. (The Yankees lost the game 9 to 8.)

In 1950, Berra tied the major-league record for passed balls. But between July 28, 1957, and May 18, 1959, Berra played 148 consecutive games without an error. He was now acknowledged the best catcher in the league, both defensively and at bat. In 1952, he set the record (30) for home runs by a catcher.

Because Berra appeared awkward and had a slightly knock-kneed stride, some observers thought him slow. But he was really one of the fastest men at his position, a fine base-runner, and quick to back up throws. He had been a soccer player in St. Louis and had developed his speed and agility there.

Yogi was sometimes said to own the biggest "strike zone" in baseball. He would swing at almost any pitch he could reach and would hit it wherever it would go. Many of his long blows were driven to left field, although he batted left-handed.

Berra was named manager of the New York Yankees in 1964, led them to a pennant, lost the World Series to St. Louis, and was fired by the Yankees, who had been looking for a "character" to replace Casey Stengel on the sports pages and not just for a winning manager. Yogi promptly signed on with the New York Mets as coach. In 1972, he moved in as manager on the death of Gil Hodges.

**LOUIS BOUDREAU** started his major-league career as a third baseman with Cleveland, soon became the regular Cleveland shortstop, and before he was through had played every infield position, including catcher, and had grown into the job of playing manager. Lou was not a home-run hitter. Two-baggers were his specialty. But, in leading the club to the 1948 pennant, Lou showed the way at bat by hitting 18 home runs and attaining an average of .355—the highest of his career. He always did best as a player when he was under pressure. But once he left the field and tried to manage from the bench, he was no longer able to lift his club to the heights.

For a long time, Lou Boudreau was considered the best-fielding shortstop in the league. He ranged right and left to make incredibly difficult stops and possessed a strong and accurate arm. He was also an innovator. The "Boudreau shift," which he devised to keep Boston's Ted Williams from driving safe hits through the infield, stymied Williams for a time and was quickly imitated by other managers. But Boudreau's shift was the most daring of all—with the third baseman abandoning his position completely and playing close to second base, while the shortstop played on the "wrong" side of second.

Lou was a catcher in school, but his father, a semipro player, turned him into a third baseman. Lou's best sport, however, was basketball and his first managing experience came when he organized and managed a basketball club, while he was still in his teens. Passed up by the Chicago White Sox, Lou attended the University of Indiana with the assistance of the Cleveland Indians management, who paid Lou a monthly stipend in return for his agreement to sign with the Cleveland ball club when he graduated. Discovery of the deal brought Lou's college athletic career to a close in his junior year and Lou promptly joined the Indians. He played one season at Cedar Rapids, then joined the big club in 1938.

The Cleveland third baseman in 1938 was Ken Keltner, a solid hitter and fielder and a durable player who had just cost Cleveland $25,000. He was not about to be benched in favor of a college-boy rookie. So Lou became a shortstop. He spent part of the 1939 season with the Buffalo Bisons, and came back to Cleveland in August. He was an immediate sensation—because of his size, his grace, his speed, and his aggressiveness. His very presence on the field gave the whole club a lift and he quickly became a favorite of the fans, despite a lack of great power at the plate.

Lou's batting improved steadily and his fielding remained sensational. Before he had completed 2 seasons with the club, he was the acknowledged field leader with his spirit, his quick judgment, and his refusal to accept defeat. There was open rebellion on the club against the manager, Oscar Bitt, but Lou, because he was still counted a rookie, was not taken into the circle of rebels and stayed clear of the dissension. Two years later, when he was just 24 years old, he was named manager himself. He had always been the captain of every school and college team he had played on. This filled out his record. The war promptly interrupted his career, but when he had got all his stars back together again, Boudreau led the club to its first American League pennant in more than 20 years.

Let go by Bill Veeck, an incurable back-seat manager himself, Lou took over the managership of the Boston Red Sox. In that graveyard for managers, Lou lasted 3 seasons, in which he lifted the club from sixth place to fourth. He put in 3 seasons as manager of Kansas City and 1 as boss of the Chicago Cubs before retiring from the game.

**ROY CAMPANELLA,** when first offered a job as a catcher by Branch Rickey, boss of the Brooklyn Dodgers, did not want to accept. He was a star then (1945) with the Baltimore Elite Giants and he thought Rickey planned to use him with the Brooklyn Brown Bombers, an all-black club that existed only on paper. Campy earned $3000 a year with the Elite Giants and fattened his income by playing all winter in the Carribean League. He was happy where he was. A few days later, Campy learned from Jackie Robinson that Rickey had really wanted to sign him to a Dodger contract. So before Campy left to play ball in Venezuela that winter, he wrote to Rickey and told him where he would be. Rickey promptly invited him to report to the Brooklyn office next March.

In the spring, Campy was playing on the Dodger farm club in Nashua, N.H. Here, in 113 games, Campy batted

Lou Boudreau got into the habit of
taking charge when he captained his
school basketball team.

If Earle Combs had had a strong
throwing arm he might have been the
greatest centerfielder ever. He
owned all the other skills.

Campy always said he would not quit the game until they "cut the uniform off me". A tragic auto accident ended his career.

.290 with 13 home runs. He also impressed manager Walt Alston with his great skill behind the bat, his readiness to throw to any base, and his all-around baseball knowledge. When Alston was not on the job, he let Campy do the managing. Nashua won the league championship that year and Campy was promoted to Montreal in the triple-A International League.

Campy actually joined the Brooklyn club in 1948 as an outfielder, spent most of the time on the bench, and was sent to join Walter Alston as a catcher in St. Paul. Here Campy hit 8 home runs in his first 7 games and wiped out the last vestige of anti-black feeling in the park. On June 30, he was ordered back to Brooklyn. He had an average of .325, with 13 home runs, in just 35 games with St. Paul.

In Brooklyn, Campy hit 2 singles and a double in his first game and became a regular. He led the league in double plays by catchers that year and showed great skill in handling the wild men on the pitching staff. In 1949, his first full season in the majors, Campy was named on the All-Star team. That season he batted .287, with 22 home runs and 81 runs batted in.

Campanella played in Brooklyn 10 seasons and starred in five World Series. In 1953, he led the league with 142 runs batted in. But he was most admired by his teammates for his skill at picking runners off base. In the 1949 World Series, his first, Campy picked Phil Rizzuto off third base and left the Yankee shortstop gasping. "First time that ever happened to me!" Phil said.

No one ever loved the game of baseball more than Roy Campanella did. He infected everyone around him with his joy in the game, never balked at catching two games on the same day, and vowed that they would have to "cut my uniform off" to get him out of baseball. But an auto accident in 1957 left Roy partly paralyzed and ended his playing days forever. His fame still lives in Brooklyn, however, where he is remembered as the best catcher Ebbetts Field ever saw—smart, aggressive, cheerful, strong-armed, mighty at the plate, and a solid stay for the entire pitching staff.

**EARLE BRYAN COMBS** came from one of the closest-knit, if not the largest, families in Kentucky. Annual Combs family reunions invariably draw several hundred and would draw more than a thousand if all could find transportation. The family has its own newspaper—not a mimeographed sheet, but a full-size, professional paper, with cartoons and editorials, devoted to family affairs.

But Earle devoted himself early to baseball. At the age of 24, he had become a star with the Louisville club, managed by Joe McCarthy. Joe talked the New York Yankees, in 1923, into buying him for $50,000. Combs was one of the last of Yankee stars to be purchased outright from the minors, but no one ever regretted the expenditure, for grayhaired Earle became one of the finest lead-off men in all of baseball. A gracious, quiet-mannered man, he immediately made a place for himself in the Yankee dream outfield between Ruth and Meusel.

Combs resembled Kiki Cuyler in that he seemed to have all the skills. He was extremely fast afoot, a sharp judge of fly balls, quick to learn the habits of hitters, and an aggressive, powerful hitter. His only weakness—and it was a serious one—was his lack of a throwing arm. He could cover almost the whole outfield, from foul line to foul line, but he had trouble getting the ball back to the bases. Fortunately, his two mates, Ruth and Meusel, owned cannonlike arms.

Combs's first full season with the Yankees was one of his best. In 1925, in 150 games, he batted .342 and made 401 putouts in centerfield. In 1927, when the greatest Yankee team of all was finally put together, Combs reached his high mark. He led the league in hits, with 231, and in triples, with 23. His batting average was .356. He topped all centerfielders in the league with 411 putouts. In the World Series that year, when the Yanks defeated the Pirates in 4 games, Earle scored 6 runs. His final run, made in the ninth inning of the fourth game on a passed ball, won the World Championship. Earle also set a World Series outfield record that year by making 16 putouts in 4 games.

Before the 1928 World Series, Combs, who had hit .310 in the season and led the league in doubles, broke a finger and had to stay on the bench. But in the final game, in the seventh inning, Manager Huggins let Earle go to bat, bandage and all, in place of Benny Bengough. Earle, who was sometimes called the Kentucky Rosebud because of the neatness of his demeanor, lined out a long sacrifice that brought in a run.

In the 1932 World Series, Combs outdid himself by driving in 4 runs and scoring 8 in the 4 games. His average for this series, the last he was to play in, was .375. In 1934, in pursuit of a long fly ball, Earle smashed into the centerfield fence in St. Louis and fractured his skull. This was the last time he ever hit over .300. He played one more season, then retired from active play with a lifetime average of .325. He spent the next several years as a coach with the Yankees, the Browns, and the Red Sox.

## STANLEY ANTHONY COVELESKI, although he led the American League in strikeouts in 1920, did not believe in trying to fan batters. "Why should I pitch 7 or 8 balls to a batter," he would ask, "when I can get him out on one?" Stan was not looking for records during his 14-year career. He just wanted to win ball games. And his control was so exquisite that he sometimes retired the side on 3 or 4 pitches. He won 3 World Series games for Cleveland in 1920, pitching 9 full innings in each. In the first game, he threw only 72 pitches. In the second, 78. In the third, 82.

But when Stan needed strikeouts, he could get them. In a game against Washington, when Sam Rice opened up with a triple, Stan struck out the next 3 batters. The first batter in the second inning got a two-base hit. Whereupon, Stan struck out the second and third batters and got the fourth to pop up. These were his only strikeouts in the game. Pitching against Philadelphia in Cleveland, and leading by 1 run in the ninth, Stan struck out the side. He liked to

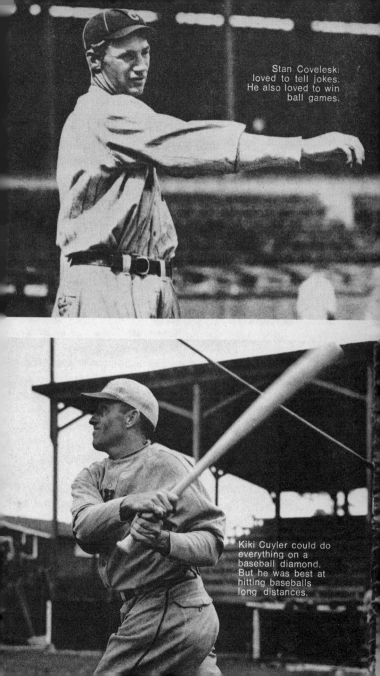

Stan Coveleski loved to tell jokes. He also loved to win ball games.

Kiki Cuyler could do everything on a baseball diamond. But he was best at hitting baseballs long distances.

finish up a game in a hurry and sometimes completed the whole 9 innings in less than an hour.

Stan was a workhorse, too. He hardly ever, while he was top man on the Cleveland staff, took more than 2 days' rest between assignments. He did, however, once require 3 days off, after beating the Yankees in 19 innings, 3 to 2. After the extra day off, Covey trimmed the Chicago club by the same score.

In 1912, Stan's brother Harry first recommended Stan to the Phillies, the club Harry worked for, but Stan, after winning 2 games of the 5 he worked in, was judged not ready for the majors. Four years later, when he was 26, he joined the Cleveland club, which was just getting used to being called the Indians, in the American League. A steady, soft-spoken man who liked jokes and never seemed to lose his temper, Stan almost immediately became the mainstay of the Cleveland staff.

## HAZEN SHIRLEY "KIKI" CUYLER was, without question, one of the dozen greatest ball players of all time. Like the other greats—Cobb, Ruth, Wagner, Speaker, Sisler, Mays, Clemente—he could do just about everything for a baseball club. He hit often and hit hard. He had great speed, could judge a fly or line drive in an instant, and could come in or go far out to rob batters of hits. He was an excellent base-runner and owned one of the strongest and most accurate arms in the game. No wonder Pittsburgh fans, after he had played in their outfield for 2 seasons, began to call him "the new Ty Cobb".

Cuyler joined the Pittsburgh club in 1921, when both he and the century were 21 years old. He did not become a regular, however, until 1924. That year, he hit .354. Next year he hit .357. In 1926, he hit .321 in 157 games. There were other great players and future Hall of Famers on that club then: Pie Traynor, Joe Cronin, and the Waners. But the favorite of all the fans was Kiki, whose mighty bat was counted on to bring the pennant to Pittsburgh in 1927.

The Pirates did win the pennant in 1927, but Cuyler played a very small part in winning it. He appeared in only 85 games. In the spring, he had been in a slight batting slump—hitting over .300, but still in a slump compared to his pace in previous years. In June, he injured an ankle sliding into third. There was talk then that he might be traded off for a pitcher.

He and his manager had been in frequent sharp disagreement over Kiki's spot in the batting lineup. Manager Donie Bush placed him second, but Cuyler wanted to hit third, because he had no confidence in his hit-and-run ability. In 1925, batting third, he had driven in 125 runs. Just the same, when Kiki got back in the game, he immediately hit a triple and 2 singles.

Then, in a game against the Giants, Kiki was out at second on a play in which he did not slide. Bush fined him $50 and put him on the bench. And there Kiki stayed. Even in the World Series, with the Yankees beating the Pirates, Cuyler was kept on the bench, although he was healthy and eager to play, while the outraged fans kept roaring "We want Cuyler!" Next year, Cuyler was sent to the Cubs.

Kiki played 8 years in Chicago and proved that his skills had not deteriorated. In only 2 seasons did his average fall below .300, and he led the league in stolen bases 3 times. In 1929, when the Cubs won the pennant, Kiki hit .360 with 43 stolen bases and 102 runs batted in. He led all right-fielders in the league with 288 putouts. The Cubs lost the World Series to the Athletics but Kiki, with 6 hits and 4 runs batted in, maintained his reputation as a clutch player. (He broke up the deciding game of the 1925 World Series with a double that cleared the bases.)

**BILLY EVANS,** throughout the early years of the 20th century, and on into baseball's Golden Years (1920's), dominated the umpires in the American League as Bill Klem did in the National League. A handsome, well-built, well-spoken, literate and polished gentleman, Evans was as sharp in calling balls and strikes as Bill Klem ever was. He was every bit as confident a decision maker as Klem was too. And like Klem he was never ashamed to ask for help when he had not seen a play.

Once, in the World Series of 1909, when Detroit faced Pittsburgh, and he and Bill Klem worked the series together, they **both** missed sighting a ball that Pittsburgh's Dots Miller had driven into the temporary bleachers at Pittsburgh. (Each had expected the other to call it.) So Billy asked the fans (who were all calling "home run"!) just where the ball had landed. And when they showed him where it had bounced in fair ground and caromed into the bleachers, he, with Klem's approval, emphatically ruled it a grounds-rule double. And after that, Billy Evans suggested that the alternate umpires, instead of merely sitting in the seats to watch the game, be stationed on the foul lines to call such plays. His suggestion was adopted.

Billy differed from Klem in that he had complete control of his temper. He was as likely to turn off a protesting ballplayer with a soft answer as to throw the man out of the game and could laugh at a sarcastic crack that would redden the neck of a colleague. When a husky New York pitcher once walked up to Billy to ask, "What's the daily quota for missed balls and strikes allowed to you guys anyway?" Billy looked the man calmly in the eye and replied, "Oh, about a dozen."

But when Ty Cobb, one day in Cleveland, outraged at some imagined wrong Billy had done him, challenged Evans to "meet me under the grandstand" Billy was right there. Despite Cobb's stranglehold on Billy's necktie, Evans fought the big man even until the two were pulled apart.

Very few ballplayers really disliked Evans, although some had a running feud with all umpires on general principle. Indeed, most ballplayers rejoiced when they heard that Billy would work their game. They knew that the pitcher could then nick the corners of the strike zone and still earn

Billy Evans dominated the umpires in the American League during Baseball's Golden Years.

strikes. And they knew no batter was going to be called out on a neck-high pitch.

In his spare time, Billy was a sports writer, with a ghost to help him. He wrote a syndicated sports column and contributed articles to **Sporting News.** When he was through as an umpire he was named general manager of the ballclub in Cleveland, a city where he had won many friends in high places.

# FORD CHRISTOPHER FRICK was the first commissioner of baseball to come out of the baseball business. His predecessors, Judge Kenesaw M. Landis and Senator Albert B. Chandler, had been national figures chosen to lend a quasi-public character to the national game. Frick was an insider, selected to preside over the rapid expansion of the baseball business. The era of his commissionership was a

sort of era of good feeling, with a minimum of friction, and no abrasive enforcement of the rules governing the swapping, purchasing, and assigning of players. Indeed, under Frick's regime, ways were often sought to make rules self-enforcing, so there would be no investigators from the commissioner's office to give club owners sleepless nights.

Ford Frick founded the National Baseball Hall of Fame at Cooperstown and presided over the extension of major-league baseball from coast to coast. A newspaper writer and radio broadcaster to begin with, Frick was always concerned with the spreading of the baseball gospel. After leaving **The New York Journal,** where he had been the top baseball writer, Frick joined the public-relations staff of the National League. In 1934, he became president. He took the league through some critical times, none more critical than the ultimate breaking of the unwritten ban on black ballplayers. It was ironic that Frick actually took part in a meeting when club owners voted 15 to 1 that signing of black players would endanger their investments, and that he distributed the resolution for adoption of that stand. (Branch Rickey voted against it.) For it was Frick's forth-right statement, threatening lifetime suspension, that brought to an abrupt end a planned strike of white ball-players to prevent the signing of Jackie Robinson.

Frick's gentle manners and his skill at keeping baseball's face shining in public persuaded the club owners to make him commissioner, despite some feeling that that job "belonged" to a figure outside the baseball hierarchy, who could act as impartial arbiter in all matters affecting the interests of the players or the public. Frick's ability to keep the peace among the owners, to oppose certain movements among the players, and to win the hearts of the fans made it clear that the commissionership could become a sort of super-presidency completely under the control of the owners and with no need to place life-or-death power in the hands of a man whose loyalties did not rest with those who paid his salary.

Ford Frick had been a baseball
broadcaster and sportswriter before
he became National League president
and then commissioner.

Jim Galvin threw harder than any pitcher
of his day. He never used a curve.

**JAMES F. GALVIN** was always called "Pud"—for the same reason that bald men are called "Curly," because Jimmy was anything but a soft touch. In the 1880s the word for a soft touch was "puddin," usually shortened to "pud". A stocky Irish lad from the St. Louis "Kerry Patch," Galvin was one of the strongest pitchers alive. He had neither curve nor change of pace and specialized in blowing his fast ball right past the batters. His sturdy, rapid way of working, and his perfect control, earned him the added nickname of "Little Steam Engine." He was also one of the first pitchers to concentrate on keeping base-runners close to the bag. He never wanted anyone to reach base on him and if they did he would not rest until he had found a way to get them off the lines. He developed a tricky motion that was not quite a balk, but that kept base-runners bewildered.

Jimmy Galvin, along with a Kerry Patch neighbor named Tim Sullivan, a catcher, started out in baseball as a full-time "amateur" with the various fast nines in his home city, and joined the St. Louis Reds when the club turned professional in 1873. He and Sullivan won fame as the Kerry Patch Battery. In 1876, with the Reds, Galvin pitched 2 no-hit games, 1 against the Cass Club of Detroit, a traveling nine named after Lewis Cass, perennial Democratic candidate from Michigan.

The St. Louis Reds folded up before the 1876 season was over and Galvin moved to the Pittsburgh Alleghenies, who joined the International Association, the first minor league, in that year. But Jim really did his finest work for the Buffalo club in the National League. He joined them in 1878, teaming up with still another Kerry Patch catcher named Dolan, and became the workhorse of the nine. Season after season, he and Dolan would appear as the Buffalo battery in every other game. Two years in a row he won 46 games and in 10 years he won more than 20 each season. In 1880, he pitched a no-hit game for Buffalo against Worcester, a major-league club in those days. In 1883, he pitched another no-hitter against Detroit.

Solid and strong, weighing 190 pounds, the rugged right-hander stayed in the major leagues for 14 seasons. In 1885 he joined the Pittsburgh club of the American Association (then a major league) and was still pitching for Pittsburgh the following season when the club entered the National League. Here he was teamed with catcher Doggie Miller to form another invincible battery.

In his big-league career, Jimmy Galvin pitched 5,959 innings and won 365 games. Like most pitchers of his day, Jim, who earned through his gentle ways, the added nickname of "Gentleman Jeems," also played the outfield or infield when he was not pitching, so he played a great deal more baseball than most of the pitchers who share the honors with him in the Hall of Fame. Jim ended his career where it began, pitching for St. Louis, at the age of thirty-six, in 1892.

# JOSH GIBSON was perhaps the mightiest home-run hitter who ever lived. And there are many who saw both Gibson and Babe Ruth who will still give the medal to Josh. Josh never played in the major leagues and so his records have not been so fondly recorded as Ruth's have been. But during his days in the National Negro League, he surely hit no fewer than 600 home runs. And he hit at least 80 in 1 season.

As Satchel Paige used to advertise his strikeouts in advance, so would Josh Gibson predict his home runs. He would promise 2 in a game or 4 in a game and nearly always make good on his promises. Nor was there ever anything freakish about the blows he hit. They carried far beyond the fences in big-league parks—and he played in many of them. Besides, he was one of the smartest and strongest catchers who ever performed, able, it was said, to cut down a stealing runner at second base without ever coming out of a crouch. When he and Roy Campanella played on the same team, as in a game between black All-Star clubs, there was never any argument over who

Josh Gibson was perhaps the greatest hitter who ever played baseball. He hit more home runs in big-league parks than any other player in history.

Vernon Gomez was said to be "faster than Lefty Grove". But his slow curve was a killer too.

would play behind the plate. Josh would be the catcher and Campy would play third base.

Walter Johnson watched Josh Gibson catch one day and insisted he was better than Bill Dickey. "He could catch in a rocking chair," Walter said. "If he were white almost any club would pay a quarter million dollars for him."

But it was for his hitting rather than his defensive skill that Josh was prized. He was no "country-fair-type" hitter, cow-tailing his bat at everything he could reach. Josh had a smooth, level swing and an aggressive style. Like Ted Williams, he attacked any pitch he liked and set out to drive it as far as it would go.

Gibson, a native of Georgia who grew up in Pittsburgh, joined the Pittsburgh Crawfords in 1927 and moved to the Homestead Grays in 1930. He performed some of his finest feats with the Grays. Most notable perhaps was his hitting 4 home runs in 1 game in 1938, at Griffith Stadium in Washington, a tough park to get a fair ball out of. In 1943, he hit 3 home runs in 1 game at the same park. Altogether, aiming at the distant left-field fence there, he put 11 balls out of the park in 1 season. No major-league player ever accomplished that.

Josh always felt that he, rather than Robinson, should have been selected as the first black player to enter the majors. Robinson had never made the mark Josh had made, could never hit the ball so far, and could not offer such a combination of skills as Josh possessed. And in 1945, Josh was still strong, active, and full of base hits. He brooded on his failure to win recognition and some said this shortened his life, for he was only thirty-five when he died in 1947. So far, there has been no player, black or white, to match him.

**VERNON LOUIS GOMEZ** was not a man given to bragging of his skills. He took himself seriously only when he was working on the mound. Off the diamond, he laughed at his own hitting ability (which was just about zero) and credited relief pitcher Johnny Murphy for making him a winner. But when he was pitching, Gomez was a fierce competitor with all the skills a man needed to get batters out in the big leagues.

Gomez came to the Yankees in 1929 from the San Francisco Seals of the Pacific Coast League where he had struck out 331 batters in 2 seasons. A power pitcher like that is supposed to be big and strong, with mighty shoulders like Dazzy Vance, or squat and solid like Jack Chesbro, or generously muscled like Walter Johnson. Gomez, however, was almost spindly. He had large hands and feet, made to seem twice their size by the slender, almost meatless, limbs they were attached to. There was nothing at all in his appearance or his mild manner to suggest the smashing speed he could provide to a pitch.

Gomez did not immediately make good with the Yankees (he had a habit of winding up with men on base) and he was deep in the dumps when he was sent down to St. Paul for seasoning. He fretted as much about his hitting as his pitching. At St. Paul, he improved his control and learned how to field his position. But he never did learn to hit, although he studied at it every day. "I tried to knock dirt out of my spikes," he said about himself in later years, "the way the big hitters did. And I cracked myself in the ankle and broke a bone!"

But he won 8 games for St. Paul in 1930 and came back to New York to become a star. Starting in June 1931, Gomez won 21 games, while losing 9, and struck out 150 batters. In 1932, when he won 24 games and lost only 7, he pitched his first World Series game against the Chicago Cubs. He gave up 9 hits, but only 1 run and struck out 8. The Cubs proclaimed him a better pitcher than Lefty Grove.

Gomez may not have been as fast as Grove, although some who faced both said he was faster. But he did have a greater variety of pitches. His slow curve, which he could place just where he wanted to, was his best pitch. He had a fine change-up to go with his fiery fast ball, so even the best batters could not time his pitches.

Lefty's finest year in the majors came in 1934, when he led the American League in wins (26), in percentage (.839), in earned run average (2.33), in complete games (25), in total innings pitched (281 and 2/3), and in strikeouts (158). Unhappily, the Yankees did not take the pennant that year, so Lefty did not pitch in a World Series.

He did make it to the World Series in 1936, 1937, 1938, and 1939, however. Altogether, he pitched in 6 World Series games and won them all. (In 1939, he did not become the pitcher of record in the only game he worked. He pitched 1 inning, allowed 3 hits, and 1 run.)

In 13 seasons with the Yankees, Gomez had only 1 losing season, his first, when he lost 5 while winning 2. In 1940, when he was out most of the year with a sore arm, he broke even, 3 and 3. In 1943, he was traded to the Washington Senators. After working in just 1 game, which he lost, he retired from active play and took to selling sporting goods. And one of his fondest memories concerned a day in 1934, his best year. But it was not a pitching victory he recalled: he got 4 hits in 1 game!

**LEON ALLEN "GOOSE" GOSLIN** was a man who could be counted on to deliver a hit when a hit was needed. He was solid, strong, and awkward-looking. In the outfield, he could barely hold his job on his defensive skills, for he lacked both speed and grace. But his arm was strong and his bat was stronger. The tougher the pitcher, the more tense the situation, the more aggressive the Goose became.

Goose wanted to be a pitcher when he first came into organized ball in 1920 with Columbia in the Sally League, but he hit too well to be kept out of the lineup, so he was sent into the outfield to stay. In his first full season with Washington, 1922, Goslin hit .324. His average did not fall below .300 until 1929, when he hit .288. Next year he was sent to the St. Louis Browns, where he immediately started batting over .300 again. In 1933, he came back to spend 1 more season at Washington, batted .299, and was shipped next year to Detroit.

In 1935, Goslin became an instant hero in Detroit when he delivered the hit that won the deciding World Series game and gave Detroit its first World Championship since the American League was founded. Goslin's winning blow was typical of him. It was the last of the ninth, with the winning run on second base, 2 out, and the count, 1 strike against him. Goslin had just driven a sharp line drive into the stands, foul. The next pitch he met with far less force— just dumped it over the second-baseman's head and won the game with it. That's all that ever counted with Goslin, bringing in those runs. And that night, crowds marching through the streets of Detroit were yelling again and again, "Yea, Goose!" as they had done a few years earlier in Washington.

Goslin was always at his best in the World Series, for that was when the pressure was on. In the 1924 World Series, when Washington played the New York Giants, Goslin hit 3 home runs in 32 times at bat. In the fourth game, the Goose made 4 hits in 4 at-bats, 1 of them a 3-run homer.

Next year, in the World Series against Pittsburgh, Goslin hit 3 more home runs, along with a double and 4 singles, in 26 at-bats.

After seventeen seasons in the majors, Goose Goslin came back to the spot where he first won his fame and ended his major-league career in Washington, where he played in only a few games and appeared 18 times as a pinch-hitter. He was 37 years old now and his batting eye had lost much of its accuracy. But he was still a bad man for a pitcher to face when there were runners ready to score. Before hanging up his uniform for keeps, the Goose put in 2 more seasons of minor-league ball, with Trenton, and managed to hit .324 in 1939.

In the majors, Goose Goslin 3 times hit 3 home runs in a game. And he drove in 100 runs or more in 11 different seasons.

Goose Goslin, after
he was supposedly
all through in
Washington, went
to Detroit to win
some crucial
ball games.

Chick Hafey, who
used to scare third
basemen with his
fierce line drives,
was one of the first
outfielders to wear
spectacles.

Jesse Haines stayed
with the St. Louis
Cardinals long
enough to become
"Pop" Haines. He
pitched until he was
past 44.

**CHARLES JAMES "CHICK" HAFEY,** from Berkeley, California, was the terror of third basemen in the National League because of his habit of driving the ball with frightening power down the left foul line. Only Jimmy Foxx, in the American League, ever hit such drives any harder. They were not line drives, said one observer, but chain lightning. But Chick, who was one of the first outfielders to wear eyeglasses on the playing field, was not especially terrifying in appearance. He was tall and strong, but weighed only 185 pounds, with nothing of the "beast" about him.

Chick might have played more baseball than he did had he not been bothered all through his career with sinus trouble. Even so, he lasted 13 seasons in the majors, with part of 2 seasons and 1 full season on the sidelines. He was a great fielder as well as a powerful hitter. His throws, like his base hits, were straight, swift, and long.

Starting with the Cardinals when he was just 21, Chick developed gradually into a top hitter. His line drives did not often clear the fences. But, as his timing improved, he began to produce a respectable number of home runs. In 1929, he hit 29 of them and drove in 125 runs. In 1931, when he led the Cardinals to the fourth pennant they had won since he joined them, Chick topped all the batters in the league with the best average of his career: .349. The Cardinals that year were perhaps the greatest club St. Louis had ever seen. They led the league from April on and took the pennant by 13½ games. Then, with Pepper Martin's help, they took the favored Athletics in the World Series, 4 games to 3. Chick, however, had done all his good work in the regular season and hit only 4 singles in the series. Chick needed hot weather to do his best. Next year he was sold to Cincinnati.

In Cincinnati, Chick suffered severely from his sinus trouble. In 1932, he was able to play in only 83 games. But he batted .344 for that stretch. Chick Hafey played in the first major-league night game in history in Cincinnati, but he did not thrive in the evening dews and damps. In 1935, his sinus pains grew unbearable and one June day he walked away from the club, leaving only a note to his room-mate saying he would not be back. He spent the rest of that year and all of 1936 at home in Walnut Creek, California, nursing his illness. In 1937, he came back to give it another try. But he was able to play in only 89 games and his average dropped to .261, his lowest since his first year in the majors. Still, he had hit so consistently in his many good years that he wound up his career with a lifetime average of .317.

## JESSE JOSEPH "POP" HAINES started ptiching major-league baseball in 1918 when he was just 24 years old and he kept it up until he was past 44, with one season in the minors because the Cincinnati Reds saw no future for him. Jesse did not become "Pop" until he was a veteran with the St. Louis Cardinals, who found him pitching for Kansas City of the American Association in 1919 and took him aboard. Branch Rickey needed only one look at the big right-hander's sharp curve and smoking fast ball to realize that Haines was a big leaguer.

Jesse had pitched just 5 innings for the Reds (in which he gave up 5 hits). In his first year with the Cardinals, he worked in 47 games, more than any other pitcher in the league, completed 19 of them and won 13, striking out 120 batters. But Jesse was not a strikeout specialist. He usually struck out more men than he walked. But his snapping curve most often resulted in infield outs.

Jesse was a workhorse all his career. In 1927, his eighth year with the Cardinals, he pitched 25 complete games out of 36 he started and won 24. Earlier in his career he had pitched a no-hit game against the Boston Braves, but he usually conserved his energy and did not throw many low-hit games. He simply took care that the enemy did not score runs enough to win. In his later years he developed a knuckle ball—a real knuckler, not a fingertip pitch—that became his most effective weapon and, by requiring minimum strength, enabled Jesse to lengthen his years of service.

But it was Jesse's knuckler that robbed him of the hero's role in the 1926 World Series. He was strangling the Yankee hitters in the final game, after giving up a third-inning home run to Babe Ruth and yielding a run in the sixth. In the seventh, he rubbed the knuckle raw, overworking his get-them-out pitch on Lou Gehrig, after he had Lou down 2 strikes to nothing. He tried his low knuckler 3 times on Lou and missed the strike zone each time. Then Hornsby ordered Lou put on base and he came out to take a look at Haines. When he saw the bleeding knuckle, Hornsby called in Grover Cleveland Alexander, who quickly made himself a hero by striking out Tony Lazzeri. Haines got credit for the win, but Alexander got the glory. Jesse also had gained credit for winning the second game, when he pitched 3 hitless innings in relief.

# WILLIAM HARRIDGE entered professional baseball wearing a stiff collar and over his own protests. He had laid the foundation of a successful career in the railroad business as a clerk with the Wabash Railroad when, at the age of 26, he was assigned to work in the office of the American League as a representative of the railroad, laying out travel schedules. Ban Johnson, president of the American League, liked young Harridge's trim appearance and tend-to-business attitude and asked the boss of the Wabash if young Will could come work steadily for the league. Harridge felt no aptitude for a baseball job. "I never played the game," he protested, "and know nothing about it."

That made no difference to Johnson, who was no baseball player either. He took Harridge on as his personal secretary. In 1927, when Johnson was eased into retirement and Ernest S. Barnard took over as president, Will Harridge was chosen secretary. Barnard died in office in 1931 and Harridge became president. He stayed in the job longer

Will Harridge gave up a promising
railroad career to go into baseball,
a game he had never played.

Harry Hooper hit from a wideopen
stance and could cover half
the outfield if need be.

even than Johnson had—26 years, from 1931 to 1959. Then, at the age of 73, having been elected and re-elected 5 times, he resigned his job and became chairman of the board.

Harridge was a strong president, but never a flamboyant one. His pleasant, quiet manner concealed an iron devotion to discipline. During his tenure, he several times had to face down some of the most powerful club owners, as he sought to impose punishment on players who had been guilty of gross misbehavior on the playing field.

In 1932, he laid a heavy fine on Manager Lew Fonseca of the White Sox and 4 of his players who had been accused of attacking an umpire. A short time later, catcher Bill Dickey of the Yankees, in a free-for-all at the Washington baseball park on the Fourth of July, broke the jaw of outfielder Carl Reynolds. To lift Bill Dickey, the best catcher in baseball, out of the New York lineup in midseason, when the struggle was hottest, might have cost the Yankees the pennant. But Harridge, without a moment's hedging, and despite the howls of Yankee boss Jake Ruppert, suspended Dickey for 30 days and fined him $1,000. (The Yankees won the pennant anyway.)

Throughout Harridge's career, he imposed fines freely, as his first boss Ban Johnson had, on players who abused his umpires or indulged in rowdy acts on the diamond. He was no grouch, no Puritan, and no sorehead (he ultimately appointed Lew Fonseca to the job of league director of promotion), but Will was determined that the league should present a clean face to the public—just as he had been raised to do back home in Indiana.

# HARRY BARTHOLOMEW HOOPER, old-time base-ball fans would argue, was a member of the real "dream" outfield—not the 1927 Yankees, consisting of Meusel, Combs, and Ruth—but the one that played in Boston in the early 1900s: Lewis, Speaker, and Hooper. There is, perhaps, no doubt that, while the later Yankee outfield could outhit

the Boston boys, the trio who played in Fenway Park had no match defensively. Of the three, any one of whom could shoot down a runner from the far outfield, Harry Hooper perhaps owned the mightiest and most accurate arm. He was a right-hander of medium size, a quiet sort, swift and sure in the outfield, fast on the bases, and a steady, but never spectacular, hitter. He was usually remembered for the great catches he made, or the trolley-wire throw from right field that caught some runner trying to get to third base.

Hooper was one of several California baseball players who were scouted and signed by the club owner himself—John I. Taylor of the Boston Americans. Hooper was a college athlete, a star at St. Mary's College in Santa Clara. When Taylor first saw him, Harry was an outfielder on the Sacramento team of the "outlaw" (outside baseball's National Agreement, that is) California State League. Hooper appealed to Taylor because he was so fleet of foot, and Taylor liked to see his ballplayers run. Under his ownership, the Boston club was known as the Speed Boys, for everyone on the team was likely to steal a base. Hooper could also cover immense yardage in the outfield. He needed to, because Tris Speaker used to like to play in close behind second base, relying on speed and judgment to get the balls hit over his head. So Hooper had to take care of a good portion of deep right center.

Hooper's batting average, in his eleven-plus seasons with the Red Sox, was only twice better than .300. (He hit .311 in 1911 and .312 in 1920.) But he seldom stole fewer than 20 bases a season, and in 1910 he stole 40. He was so fast getting down to first, and so crafty at working a pitcher for a walk, that he ultimately became lead-off man for the Sox and one of the best of his era. Like Cobb, he batted on the left-hand side of the plate to get a stride closer to first, even though he was right-handed.

When Harry and his mates were patrolling the Boston outfield, enemy batters complained that it had become impossible to drive a fair ball out there and have it land safely. And the runner who thought he might make third base from first, on a deep drive to right, was too often sadly mistaken when Hooper had charge of right field. So Harry's worth to the Boston club could not be measured by his batting average.

When Harry shifted from Boston to Chicago in 1921, after the baseball had been enlivened, his batting average moved upward and he hit more home runs. Batting with a spread-legged stance and a short stride, he liked to upper-cut the ball. He achieved his top batting average of .327 in 1921, his first year with the White Sox. With the Red Sox, he did his best slugging at World Series time. In the 1912 World Series, he made 9 hits; in 4 World Series, he made a total of 24 safe blows.

Harry's most famous exploit was perhaps his spectacular catch of a certain home run off the bat of New York's Larry Doyle in the final game of the 1912 World Series. Doyle drove the ball almost on a line toward the temporary bleachers in right center. Harry took after it, leaped backward over the low fence, and grabbed the ball as he lay atop the fans. The Giants insisted that the catch was illegal. The umpires said Doyle was out.

## WAITE CHARLES HOYT of Brooklyn was a high-school hero there and first applied for a major-league job with the Dodgers. The Dodgers hardly noticed him, however (although Casey Stengel, playing for the Dodgers then, insisted he recalled the baggy baseball pants Hoyt wore to the tryout). The man who signed Hoyt to his first pro con-tract was John McGraw of the New York Giants. He sent 16-year-old Hoyt to the minors, after letting him pitch 1 inning for the Giants in which he struck out 2 men. But before Hoyt could return, McGraw had run out of options on him and let him go to the Boston Red Sox. When young Hoyt reappeared in New York, it was as a pitcher for the Yankees.

With Boston, where his best season mark was .500, Hoyt set no records. But he did pitch 11 innings against the Yankees and not grant them a hit or a run or a walk. The New Yorkers were deeply impressed by Hoyt's speed and control. He joined the Yankees when he was 21 years old, and immediately began to win victories. He was a winning pitcher in every season but 1, from 1921 to 1926. Then, in 1927, after a long serious talk with Joe McCarthy, who explained to Hoyt the difference between being good and being great, Hoyt led the league with 22 victories and only 7 defeats. Hoyt also won the only World Series game he worked in that year. In 1921, he had taken special delight in taking 2 games from John McGraw's Giants, who had ridiculed his boyish appearance.

In 1928, Hoyt won 23 games, tops of his career, then pitched 2 complete games in the World Series and won them both, striking out 14. Hoyt never again passed the 20-victory mark, but he continued to post winning seasons, even after he had been traded to Detroit and then to Philadelphia. In Philadelphia, after Hoyt had put in a few disappointing weeks with Detroit, Connie Mack made him into a winner again and Hoyt helped bring the club into the 1931 World Series, in which he pitched 6 innings and lost his only game.

A man with tremendous strength in his shoulders, who used to condition himself by running and skating in the wintertime, Hoyt lasted 20 seasons in the majors and worked in 7 World Series. He finally joined the Brooklyn Dodgers, as a 32-year-old veteran, and returned that same year to the New York Giants where he had made his start. This was Hoyt's first losing season since 1925 and he soon made up for that by winning 15 games for the Pittsburgh Pirates in 1934.

Hoyt was with the Pirates when Babe Ruth, his old teammate (and playmate), made his final appearance in Forbes Field and hit 3 home runs. Hoyt had warned his new teammates before the game that the old lion might still have a few muscles left in his mighty paw.

Waite Hoyt used to
take some ribbing
for his schoolboy
complexion—until
his mates
discovered how
tough he was
underneath.

Monte Irvin with the New York Giants
in 1951

Hoyt finished his major-league career where he had wanted to start it—with the Brooklyn Dodgers once more. He pitched his final major-league game in 1938. Hoyt did not long stay out of baseball, however. He returned as a broadcaster of games in Cincinnati and won a tremendous following throughout several states for his knowledgeable and witty commentary.

**MONTE IRVIN,** whose proper name is Monford Merrill Irvin, "wasted" his best baseball years, he said, in the Negro Leagues. But he was still a great ballplayer when he joined the New York Giants in 1949, at the age of 30. A swift, graceful, trim-looking and soft-spoken athlete, he could run, hit and throw with the best of them. Some of his contemporaries held that he was the equal of Willie Mays as a hitter. Monte himself allowed that he was "way past his peak" when he entered the major leagues. In the Negro National League, where he played infield and outfield for the Newark Eagles, he once batted .422 in a season. He also hit 41 home runs one year. Monte started his professional career at the age of 19 and played winter and summer, part of the time in the Mexican League as well as in Cuba. He also served a stretch in the Army Corps of Engineers.

Monte Irvin and Hank Thompson, who was playing with the Kansas City Monarchs of the Negro National league, joined the Giants at the same time, January, 1949—the first black players to sign with the club. They were assigned immediately to the Jersey City Giants and came up to the big team in June. Monte played in 36 games, in the outfield and at first and third base. But he could not get adjusted to big league pitching, so next year he found himself back in Jersey City. In eighteen games in the spring of 1950, Monte batted .510. Technically, there was still no room on the Giants roster for Irvin, but Manager Durocher was not going to allow a bat like that to waste its power in the minor leagues. He promptly promoted Monte again to the varsity and let him fill in whenever some outfielder was hurt or infielder grew tired. Playing at three different positions, Monte batted .299 and hit 15 home runs.

Next year, 1951, having proved himself a major leaguer, Monte was stationed at first base—the position he liked least. (He simply did not care for wild throws.) After a few weeks, Durocher, with his club fighting back from an 11-game losing streak, put Irvin back in the outfield, where he did best. Monte began to hit consistently and with power. Whether Monte inspired the club or not, or just caught fire with the rest of them, he did pace them to the pennant, with a .312 batting average, 24 home runs and 121 runs batted in. Preacher Roe, the Dodger star pitcher, said Irvin was the toughest of them all with men on base.

In the World Series against the Yankees that year, Monte put on a one-man show. In the first game, played at the Yankee Stadium, Monte hit a triple and three singles and stole home to lead the Giants to a 51 to 1 victory. In the second game, which the Yankees won, Irvin got four more hits—a double and three singles. Unfortunately, Monte could not ignite the rest of the Giants and the World Series was lost. But Irvin was the leading hitter, with an average of .458—11 hits in 24 times at bat. That was the peak of Monte's big league career, although he put in several more strong years with the Giants. In 1953 he attained his highest batting average—.329, with 21 home runs. The previous season a broken ankle had sidelined him for most of the year but he still managed to hit .310 in 46 games. Monte was traded to the Chicago Cubs in 1956 and finished his active career there. He now holds a job as special consultant to the Commissioner of Baseball.

**JOSEPH J. KELLEY'S** name has never gathered about it the lasting fame that clings to some of his Oriole teammates like John McGraw, Willie Keeler, Hughey Jennings, and Wilbert Robinson. That may have been because Joe never made a great mark as manager, although he tried it in Cincinnati and in Boston. By the time he was through as leader of the Boston Braves, however, there were still many fans who thought of him as the greatest left-fielder the game had ever known.

When Joe was 18 years old, in 1889, he was pitching for the professional baseball club in Lowell, Massachusetts, and dreaming of the day when he might make the grade with the Boston Beaneaters of the National League. But when Joe's opportunity came, in 1891, the Boston management found him not quite steady enough to share the pitching with the likes of Kid Nichols and John Clarkson, so Joe took to the outfield. For this job, Joe had everything he needed. He was a solidly built young man, just under six feet tall, well-muscled, sharp-eyed, and fast. He could fire a strike to the plate from the deep outfield and cover more than his share of the park. And he hit the ball with great authority.

Joe signed as an outfielder with Omaha and made such a mark there that he was quickly signed by the Pittsburgh club, which had just been nicknamed the Pirates. Joe hit moderately well here, but was traded after only 56 games to Baltimore, where he promptly found himself.

In his first full season in Baltimore, in 1893, Joe hit 9 home runs (a tall number for those dead-ball days) and batted .305. He also stole 33 bases. In 1894, the year the Orioles won the pennant (and the year the pitching distance was lengthened to 60 feet 5 inches), Joe batted .393 with 6 home runs and he stole 46 bases. From that time on, as long as he remained in Baltimore, Joe never batted below .300. In 1895, he stole 54 bases. In 1896, he stole 87 bases, to lead the league.

Before he had finished in Baltimore, Joe had played every infield position, and had become as sharp an exponent of "inside" baseball as manager Ned Hanlon himself. There was practically nothing that needed doing on a baseball diamond that Joe could not do. Had he chosen to stay at first base, he would have been one of the best there.

In 1899, along with Hanlon and a number of the other

Orioles, Joe moved on to Brooklyn (which was under the same management as Baltimore) and here he remained a hero at the plate and in the field. He went back to Baltimore in 1902, when Baltimore joined the American League. But there was a bidding war going on between the leagues and Joe quickly jumped his contract with the American League club to seek better pay with the Cincinnati Reds. After 2 weeks in Cincinnati, Joe was named manager. Under his leadership, the club began to win steadily. Joe contributed by batting .321 and playing several different positions in the infield and outfield. In 4 seasons, however, Joe could never bring his club in better than fourth. His own batting had fallen off now and he was no longer piling up stacks of stolen bases. He was let go finally and ended his career where he had started it, running the Boston Braves, right across the river from his boyhood home in Cambridge.

# GEORGE LANGE KELLY got his middle name from his uncle, Bill Lange, who, Bill's admirers said, might have become the greatest ballplayer alive had he not married a girl who disliked the game. (Bill had to retire from baseball when he got married.) George had a few of his uncle's skills, notably a strong arm and a mighty bat. He was taller than Bill too by a couple of inches (6 foot 4 to Bill's 6 foot 2). And George stayed in baseball until he simply grew too old to play.

Called "High-Pockets" because of the extraordinary length of his legs, Kelly played first base for the New York Giants, where he would not ordinarily have had a chance to display the strength of his throwing arm. But Manager John McGraw, who never let talent go to waste, schooled George to scamper out into the outfield on deep flies, with men on base, so the mighty Kelly arm could be used to relay long throws home to the plate. Ordinarily, the relay man undertakes to let the outfielder throw long while he throws short. George did it the other way around and fired many a cannon-shot in from far out on the grass, yards

Joe Kelley wanted to be a pitcher. He became a hard-hitting outfielder with the old Baltimore Orioles.

George "High-Pockets" Kelly played first base for the New York Giants.

away from his official position. For three years in a row (1920 to 1922) Kelly led all first basemen in the league in assists.

As a batter, George specialized in line drives. He never hit more than 21 home runs in a season but he did deliver many a hard drive with men on base and five times registered more than a hundred runs batted in. Had he been a left-handed batter he might have popped a few more four-base hits into the handy Polo Grounds right-field seats. But John McGraw liked George Kelly just the way he was. And he was for a long time acknowledged the best first baseman in the league.

The man Kelly eventually succeeded in the Giants had been named the best first baseman in baseball, a miraculous fielder and a consistent hitter—Hal Chase, the Adonis of the game. Alongside Chase, young George Kelly looked uncertain and awkward. But George always gave his best, and Chase did not. So Manager John McGraw let Chase go and helped Kelly turn himself into a slick and aggressive first baseman, whose trolley-wide throws across the diamond caught more than one reckless runner who was trying to grab an extra base.

Eventually McGraw brought Bill Terry, a pitcher-outfielder, in to get him ready to succeed long George at first base. But George refused to slow down and for a time he and Terry took turns at the base, with Kelly playing the outfield when Terry took over. In 1927, when Kelly was going on 32, McGraw sent him to Cincinnati for Edd Roush and a large sum of money. In Cincinnati, long George played a lot of second base, creating a startling impression with his beanpole height in the center of the diamond, but earning cheers by the way he could race out into centerfield to relay throws to the plate. Kelly finished his career in Brooklyn, where so many of McGraw's young heroes found themselves when they grew old.

**SANFORD "SANDY" KOUFAX,** the best pitcher in baseball in the 1960s, very nearly gave up on himself in

1958, when his club moved from Brooklyn to Los Angeles. A hard-throwing pitcher with a fine curve, he seemed unable to develop the control that would make him a winner. His salary was small. He had been in the majors 3 whole seasons and had never won more than 5 games in a season. Moving to the coast meant he would have to move out of his family's home and set himself up in an apartment of his own, cutting deep into his scanty pay.

But Sandy stuck it out, learned to pace himself more carefully, gradually achieved control so that his whistling speed and low curve could do their work, and became one of the highest-paid men in the game. In 1959, Sandy tied Bob Feller's record by striking out 18 batters in a game against the Giants. But he won only 8 games that year.

It was 1961 before Sandy really got command of his pitches. He worked in 42 ball games and, that season, won 18 of them, striking out along the way more batters than anyone else in the game—269. In 1962, he again struck out 18 batters in a game against the Cubs, but an ailment in his index finger benched him in July. In 1963, however, Sandy really terrified the enemy. Starting 40 games and completing 20, he won 25 while losing only 8, for a percentage of .833. That season, he again led both leagues with a strikeout total of 306. In the World Series that year, Sandy started, completed, and won both his games, allowing only 3 bases on balls in 18 innings.

After posting 19 victories and a league-leading percentage of .792 in 1964, Sandy led his club to another pennant in 1965, when he won 26 games out of the 43 he worked in. That year, he completed 27 games and set the all-time seasonal strikeout mark of 383. He won 2 games in the World Series, striking out 29 batters in the 24 innings he worked.

By this time, Sandy was working in almost constant pain, taking frequent pain-killing injections in his overworked left arm and thinking often of retirement. Yet, he came back in 1966 to attain his highest mark, a total of 27 victories against 9 defeats. Again, he led both leagues with 317 strikeouts.

Sandy did not become a pitcher until he was in college. As a boy in Brooklyn, he played softball and, during his last year in high school, played first base on the baseball team. The Giants first looked at him, but gave up on him because of his lack of control. Sandy, however, was determined to perfect himself. It was this urge for perfection that kept him throwing harder and harder, and getting wilder. When he finally learned to relax, he began to get batters out regularly. But he was still not satisfied.

"I always go for a shutout," he said.

Had his weary arm not given out in 1966, Sandy might have won well over 200 games in the majors. As it is, he has to be satisfied with owning the strikeout record.

## WALTER "BUCK" LEONARD played baseball in the
1930s and 1940s, and some observers said that he was a combination of Hal Chase and Lou Gehrig—that is, he played first base with all the magical grace and skill of Chase and hit the ball with Gehrig's power. But where Chase was strictly a me-first man, who was reputedly ready to do almost anything for a quick bundle of cash, Buck was a team player, cheerful, outgoing, and strictly on the level. And where Gehrig was rather a loner, Buck was gregarious and merry.

Buck, playing in the semi-dilapidated Negro leagues in the old days, where team members were granted sixty cents a day for meal money, worked his way to the top in the black leagues with a salary of $1,000 a month and all expenses. Had his skin been white, he could have earned 5 times that salary for many years, for there were few men in the country who could hit a baseball any harder.

One of the few who could was a long-time teammate, Josh Gibson. On the Homestead Grays of Pittsburgh, Gibson and Leonard were like Ruth and Gehrig, with Gibson, the home-run hitter, batting third, and Leonard, the consistent

Sandy Koufax, a soft-ball player from the streets of Flatbush, became the best pitcher in baseball when he learned control.

Buck Leonard, had he been able to play in the major leagues, would probably have been recognized as the greatest first baseman of all time.

long-ball slugger, batting fourth. Sometimes, however, they might switch around, so that Gibson would come to bat fourth—and usually with Buck Leonard on base ahead of him. That was when the club was not hitting and they wanted Buck at bat a step sooner.

Buck Leonard started playing ball for money when he lost his job in the railroad shops, at age 26. He began with the Baltimore Stars, earning hardly enough to keep from going hungry, and winding up one day in New York City where the club ran out of funds and left him broke. Buck joined the Brooklyn Royal Giants then (it was 1933), but was urged by Smoky Joe Williams, one of baseball's mightiest black pitchers, who was then a bartender in Harlem, to hook up with the best black club in the nation—the Homestead Grays. Williams got Buck an offer from the Grays and Buck went on to become a star, perhaps the second greatest hitter ever in the league.

Like most black players of his era, Buck played winter and summer, hurrying to Cuba or Puerto Rico in the cold months to join one of the Latin clubs there. He would often play over 250 games in a year and he kept at it until long after an age when most men would have retired. Like Satchel Paige, however, Buck never seemed to grow old. When he was 48, he sliced 10 years off his age and got a baseball job in Mexico. But when Bill Veeck had offered him a job with the St. Louis Browns, in 1952, Buck turned him down. He was 45 then, and even though he looked and acted 35 he felt it was too late in life to subject himself to such tough competition. He still drew a good wage out of baseball and he felt it best to wind up his career in a league where the pitchers did not throw quite so hard.

# RICHARD WILLIAM "RUBE" MARQUARD was
no rube at all. He was given his nickname to suggest he was the answer to the American League's great Rube— Eddie Waddell. A tall (6 feet, 3 inches), but not overly stout (180 pounds) young man from Cleveland, Rube had

nothing of the farmer about him. But, like the original Rube, he was powerful, left-handed, and given to throwing a baseball with all his might. When McGraw signed him, Rube was the best pitcher in the minor leagues and the price McGraw paid for him indicated his value. He cost the Giants $11,000 —the most money ever paid for a rookie, and a price almost unheard of since the day, some 21 years earlier, when Boston had paid $10,000 for Mike "King" Kelly.

Kelly, for that deal, had been named the $10,000 Beauty, after a showgirl of the day who used that title in her publicity. So young Rube Marquard (he was 18 years old in 1908, when he signed with the Giants) became the $11,000 Beauty. His publicity outdid that of Mike Kelly because, for one thing, he was in New York, where there were more papers to carry his story. But the publicity nearly did him in. Weak in the knees, his stomach aflutter from all the to-do, Rube worked just 5 innings of 1 game, allowed 6 hits, and lost the game. Next year he tried again and did so badly that one writer named him the $11,000 Lemon. Poor Rube took his failure so to heart that he set out at once to pack up and go back to Indianapolis. But McGraw promised Rube he was going to be a winner and he persuaded the boy to stay.

It was 1911, however, before the Rube justified McGraw's faith. Then he earned his price twice over by leading the league with 25 wins and only 7 losses. Rube, after leading his club into the World Series, worked in 2 games in the series but could not beat the Athletics. In the first game, he allowed but 4 hits. One, however, was a 2-run homer by Frank Baker, who earned his Home-run Baker nickname in the series. And that was enough to beat New York.

In 1912, Rube enjoyed his greatest year in the game. Starting April 11 and ending July 3, Marquard won 19 games in a row, equaling the mark set by Tim Keefe, another Giant, in 1888, a year before Rube was born. Rube always insisted he really won 20. And if modern scoring rules had been used then, Rube would indeed have been credited with a win against the Dodgers. Instead, the game was credited to Jeff Tesreau, who was knocked out of the box in the ninth. Rube relieved and put the Dodgers out, but not before the Dodgers went ahead, 3 to 2, on runs Tesreau had put on base. The Giants scored twice in the ninth to win.

In the 1912 World Series, which the Giants lost to the Boston Red Sox, Rube Marquard still put frosting on his own cake by winning 2 games, both of which he started and completed. He gave up just 2 walks in 18 innings.

Rube, after winning 24 games for McGraw in 1913, began to fade the next year, although he remained a workhorse. In 1915, after he had won 9 games and lost 8, he was traded to Brooklyn. Here, after an uncertain first season, he began to win again. He had 2 winning seasons, then a disastrous one, in which he lost 18 out of the 34 games he worked in. In 1919, a broken leg kept him sidelined most of the season, but he came back to win again, was traded to Cincinnati, and won 17 games there, then wound up his career with 4 tough seasons in Boston. An appendicitis operation in 1924 kept Rube out of action most of the season and the next year, his eighteenth in the big leagues, was his last.

# JOSEPH MICHAEL "DUCKY" MEDWICK, called

Ducky, it was said, because he walked like a duck, may not have been the toughest of the St. Louis Gas House Gang of the 1930s. But there were few in the league any tougher. Like Ed Delahanty, Ducky was a man who would swing at any ball he could reach, be it in the strike zone or a yard outside it. And when he laid the fat part of the bat on the pitch, it would fly off like a cannonball. He was no slap, poke, or place man. When he saw a ball he liked, he attacked it as if he meant to break it in two.

Medwick joined the St. Louis Cardinals in 1932, when he was not yet 21. In 26 games in the outfield, he batted .349. His first full season, 1933, Medwick, who was also called "Muscles," batted .306, hit 18 home runs, and drove in 98 runs. His average never sank that low again for 6 seasons.

Rube Marquard was no Rube. He was born in Cleveland to a family named Le Marquis.

Joe Medwick started out to be a football star. He was aggressive at the plate and on the bases too.

A high-school star from New Jersey, Medwick just missed joining the Newark club, when he was kept waiting too long for an interview and stomped out of the waiting room. In 1930, just out of high school, Medwick played for Scottsdale, in the Cardinal chain. But he may still have had hopes of playing football in college, a game in which he had also starred in high school, for he insisted on playing under an assumed name, Mickey King. But after he batted over .400 there, Medwick was moved up to Houston under his right name. (In Houston he was also awarded his nickname of Ducky.)

Two seasons of batting over .300 earned Joe his job in the majors. In 1937, he hit the peak of his career with St. Louis when he not only won the Triple Crown with 31 home runs, 154 runs batted in, and an average of .374, but led the league in runs scored, in fielding average for his position, in total hits, in total bases, in most times at bat, and in most two-base hits. His 31-homer figure was really a tie with Mel Ott of the Giants. But Ducky had actually hit 32 home runs. One was washed out when the game was declared forfeited.

Medwick was not just a slugger. He was a 100 percent baseball player who ran the bases with all the ferocity he showed at bat, and who ranged over the outfield with speed and agility. He studied the enemy hitters, played against them as well as any outfielder of his time, and could throw a man out from almost any spot in the outfield.

In the World Series of 1934, Medwick earned notoriety for his run-in with Detroit third-baseman Marv Owen. It was a fight in which not a blow was struck nor any angry contact made. Owen tried to stamp on Medwick and Medwick tried to kick back. Neither attempt succeeded. But the angry fans, by showering Medwick with fruit (which he picked up and tossed to some of his mates), held up the game until Joe had been removed.

Medwick was traded to Brooklyn in 1940 and his hitting fell off to a mere .300. In 1943 he was swapped to the

Giants, where he put in three seasons, playing a few games at first base. In 1944, after he dropped under .300 for the first time in his career, Joe came back and hit .337. From then on, the big muscles began to play out. Joe could no longer play a full season and his average dropped below .300 again. A part-time operator now, he was traded to the Braves, back again to Brooklyn, and wound up his playing career as a pinch-hitter with the Cardinals in 1947.

**STANLEY FRANK MUSIAL,** if it had not been for a minor-league manager named Dickie Kerr, himself a former pitcher for the Chicago White Sox, would have been merely a sore-armed rookie pitcher who could not make the grade. A soft-spoken, ambitious, and determined boy from a mill-town family in Pennsylvania, Stan hurt his arm while trying to make a diving catch in the outfield, where he filled in when not pitching. He was then with Daytona of the Class D Florida State League and thought that would be his last stop. But manager Dickie Kerr took the hundred-dollar-a-month rookie into his own home, along with Stan's wife and baby, and helped Stan turn himself into a hitter.

After hitting over .300 in Daytona, Stan moved rapidly up through the Cardinal chain, to Springfield, Missouri, to Rochester, New York, and in 1941 to the Cardinals, where he was destined to stay for 22 seasons. In seven of those seasons, he led his league in batting, six times in total hits, five times in runs scored, and twice in runs batted in. Stan, who seldom missed a time at bat and played in almost every game, hit hard and hit steadily, but mostly for doubles and singles. He never led the league in home runs (39 was his best, in 1948), yet he hit so steadily that when his career was over, he stood tenth in all-time home-run totals.

Stan always seemed to hit best against the Brooklyn Dodgers, where the fans, who learned to fear his appearance at the plate, named him "The Man." He never came back as a pitcher, but he turned into an able outfielder and first baseman, always ready to play anyplace his manager asked him to, if it would help the club.

Stan Musial became a great hitter after he developed this wound-up stance that enabled him to get full power into his swing.

LeRoy Satchel Paige was just short of his fiftieth birthday in this picture. He no longer owned his blazing speed, but he had all his cuteness.

278

Musial made a serious study of batting, working always to correct any weakness rival pitchers had discovered, until finally, there was hardly any pitch he could not hit. His peculiar "wound-up" batting stance, which gave him the appearance of peeking at the pitcher from behind his shoulder, was adopted after lengthy experimentation, in order to give him bat control as well as power.

Musial is one of the few players who played more than 3,000 games in the majors and, when he quit baseball, he stood second in lifetime number of times at bat. Musial once hit 5 home runs in a doubleheader. In lifetime total of hits, Musial stood second only to Ty Cobb and came in just behind Cobb and Ruth in total runs scored.

**LEROY PAIGE,** some observers said, was named Satchel because of his oversize feet, but he said it was a name he earned when he was a lad and found a way of carrying a half-dozen satchels at once for 10 cents each. There was no disagreement however among men who watched Satchel pitch, in his prime, about his ability on the mound. Even rival pitchers like Dizzy Dean and Lefty Gomez said Satch was the best of his day and probably of all time. Said Gomez: "I always thought Lefty Grove was the fastest pitcher in the leagues. And Satchel was just as fast, if not faster."

When he was young, pitching semipro ball, or working for one of the black professional clubs, Satch's fast ball was truly terrifying. It might tear the glove right off a catcher's hand, if the catcher was not prepared for him. And there were batters in those days who insisted they never saw the ball go by at all. By the time Satch reached the major leagues, with Cleveland, at the age of 42, he had lost much of his speed and was getting by on cunning and control. He had a dozen different styles of delivery, all designed to keep the batter off balance. And his control was always superb. When he "tried out" for the Cleveland Indians in 1948 by throwing pitches to Manager Lou Boudreau in a sort of private audience, Lou counted 46 strikes in 50 pitches.

Satchel Paige worked for so many different clubs in his lifetime, there is no counting them. Even he has forgotten the names of some of the places he pitched for money. He began as a semipro in Birmingham and pitched as a youth for the Birmingham Black Barons, for the Baltimore Black Sox, and for the Chicago American Giants. He also worked for a black team that played out of Cleveland, but gave its hometown as Nashville. When that team disbanded, Satch joined the Pittsburgh Crawfords and won games for them until 1933, when he was 28 years old.

Satch took time off from the Crawfords to organize a semipro club in Bismarck, North Dakota—a team that won the national semipro championship, in the tournament at Wichita, after winning 100 games and losing only 1 through the season. Satch pitched that year, in one stretch, in 29 games within 30 days. He always felt best when he worked steadily and he was always busy on the ball diamond, getting into "pepper" games, shagging flies, just running. It was this constant activity that kept him always in perfect condition. And because he pitched in the Latin leagues, he could keep busy year-round.

In 1934, the year his club won the semipro tournament, Satch had pitched a no-hitter for the Crawfords against the Homestead Grays. He also pitched in the East-West Black All-Star Game in Chicago, after traveling 1,000 miles by car. He gave up 1 hit in that game, in the ninth inning, and finally won the game 1 to 0.

When the semipro tournament was over, Satch rejoined the Crawfords to pitch before 30,000 fans at Yankee Stadium in a 1 to 1 tie. In the late thirties and early forties, Paige also pitched for many a barn-storming club against teams of major leaguers and faced most of the great major-league hitters of the day, including DiMaggio, Hack Wilson, Lou Gehrig, Johnny Mize, Charley Gehringer, and Heinie

Manush. Any of them would have counted himself lucky to get more than a scratch single off Paige.

Satchel's entry into the majors at his "advanced" age was deemed by some a joke or a circus stunt. But batters who faced him soon learned how serious he was. He won 6 games for Cleveland, while losing 1, and helped put the club in the World Series, where he worked part of an inning and sent the foe down hitless.

Satch put in 2 seasons with Cleveland and 3 with the St. Louis Browns, part of a season with Kansas City, and ended as a coach with Atlanta, in his sixties. But he had done his best pitching in the Negro leagues, and had worked, it was figured, in at least 2,500 games. One year he pitched in 134 games. And he pitched, he said (and no one could contradict him), a "hatful" of no-hitters.

# WESLEY BRANCH RICKEY, like so many crafty

baseball managers, started his career as a catcher, "working" his way through Ohio Wesleyan University on an athletic scholarship. A skinny, solemn type of youth, Rickey barely clung to a job in the big leagues, where he caught 1 game (and made no hits) for the St. Louis Browns in 1905, after having been dropped by the Cincinnati Reds in 1903 for refusing to play ball on Sunday. ("A promise to my mother," Rickey explained in later years.) Rickey played 64 games for St. Louis in 1906 and batted .284. He was then traded to the New York Highlanders (also called the Burglars) where he caught 52 games and batted .182, about 1 hit in every other game. Rickey then came down with TB, quit baseball, and, after recovering his health, set out to practice law in Boise, Idaho.

His batting average as a lawyer was about the same as it had been in the big leagues. He had a client who told young Rickey to "get the hell out of here." Branch quit law immediately and returned to baseball as assistant to the president of the St. Louis Browns. Before the season was over,

Rickey had taken over as field manager of the club, put himself into the lineup twice as a pinch-hitter (and got no hits), but still managed to boost the club from last place to fifth. His work with the Browns, a collection of sad sacks, established his reputation as a shrewd judge of talent and an aggressive manager.

Rickey was then made president of the St. Louis Cardinals where rival clubs, especially the New York Giants, grew fat on his shrewdness—by simply waiting until he had spotted a good player, and then outbidding him. This drove Rickey to his invention of the "chain-store system"—his first great contribution to the game. By establishing a long string of minor-league affiliates, Rickey assured his club of a continual flow of able rookies.

Under Rickey, the Cardinals, who had been almost as sorry a club as the Browns, turned into contenders. For a time, Rickey acted as field manager, but his work on the bench was not so effective as his front-office work, and he went back to his desk. Rickey was no namby-pamby, however. While managing, he once traded punches with his own second baseman, cross-grained Rogers Hornsby.

At St. Louis, Rickey discovered or developed many of the game's greatest stars, notably George Sisler, whom he signed off the University of Michigan campus, where Rickey had coached baseball for a time. He also brought in Sunny Jim Bottomley, Hornsby, Dizzy Dean, Chick Hafey, and Joe Medwick.

After a falling out with the Cardinal owner, Rickey came to Brooklyn as part-owner of the Dodgers. Here after first organizing a Negro league—the United States League—and putting in his own club, the Brooklyn Brown Dodgers, Rickey made his next great contribution, probably his greatest: he forced the league to open their rosters to black players. With every other owner voting against him, and only Commissioner Chandler on his side, Rickey signed Jackie Robinson and put a final end to the disgraceful "color line."

Red Ruffing, a loser with the Boston Red Sox, became a big winner in New York.

Branch Rickey never attended (or played in) a baseball game on Sunday.

Brooklyn was only a way station for Rickey, however. He ultimately sold his interest there and, at the age of 69, took over as boss of the Pittsburgh Pirates. Here, he began to see visions of even wider expansion of the game and it was he who prompted (after he had left Pittsburgh) the creation of the Continental League, with a New York entry that ultimately became the New York Mets. Asked, at 73, when he planned to retire from the game, Rickey exclaimed: "Never!" He won a championship for the Pirates before he moved on to build his new league, which never lived except on paper, but did bring National League baseball back to New York.

# CHARLES HERBERT "RED" RUFFING, unlike a
number of pitchers through the years, did not profit by accidents to his fingers. (Toad Ramsey threw a "natural" knuckle ball because of a bad finger, and Three-Fingered Brown threw a natural sinker.) Ruffing lost some toes in a mining accident and it is doubtful if this helped his effectiveness on the mound, but it did help make him tough and determined.

Red Ruffing was one of the hardest-working pitchers who ever lived. And he was ready to step in as a pinch-hitter any time they called on him. In 1930, playing for Boston and New York, Red batted .364, with 4 home runs in 40 times at bat.

Red Ruffing started his big-league career with the Boston Red Sox, where he never had a winning season, although he usually pitched more games than anyone else on the staff. In 1928 and 1929, Ruffing lost more ball games than any other pitcher in the league. But he also led the league in 1928 in number of completed games. Everyone who ever faced Red Ruffing knew he was a great pitcher who needed only some sound fielding behind him to start to win.

When Ruffing moved to the New York Yankees, he became a winner at once. He led the Yankees into the World Series 7 times, pitched in 10 World Series games, and lost only 1. He was a big, hard-throwing right-hander who never seemed to get tired. Year after year, he started in 25 or more games and always completed most of them. In 1928, he started 42 games for the Red Sox and finished 34. In 15 years with the Yankees, Red only once had a losing record. After 2 years in the armed services, however, he never recovered his youthful stamina. A knee injury in 1947 ended his career when he was with the Chicago White Sox. He had put in 22 active years in the majors.

One of the best of Ruffing's seasons came in 1937, when he led the Yankees, for the third time since he joined them, into the World Series. In his first World Series game, he had won despite allowing the enemy 10 hits. In his second World Series effort, in 1936, he had been the losing pitcher in the opening game. This time he did everything. He spread 7 hits over 9 innings. He struck out 8. He gave but 3 walks and 1 run. And he drove in 3 runs himself with a single and a double. Red was not much of a man to pitch a shutout game and he gave up plenty of hits. But he could starve the opposition to death for runs, once he had a lead to work on.

# WARREN SPAHN, according to many veteran observers, was the best left-handed pitcher in baseball history —and Spahnie would not have contradicted them. Whether he was or not, he was surely as fierce a competitor as ever lived, with an unquenchable confidence in his ability to get batters out. Even when he was long past the retirement age, Spahn would snarl angrily at being denied a chance to go once more to the mound. And he did his best pitching when his knee cartilage was so hashed up from injury that, according to the doctor who operated on it after the season was over, it looked like "chewed up crab-meat."

Bad knee or no, Warren Spahn, in 1953, the year he tore the cartilage in spring training while with the Braves, led the National League with 23 wins and only 7 losses. That was the year the Boston Braves moved to Milwaukee. Just ten years later, when Spahnie was 42 years old, he posted an identical 23-7 record for Milwaukee. Indeed he did some of his finest pitching after he turned forty. In April, 1961, five days after his 40th birthday, Spahn pitched a no-hit game against the San Francisco Giants. (He had pitched his first no-hitter just six months earlier against the Philadelphia Phillies, in September, 1960.)

Spahn, like Ted Williams, spent in the armed services the seasons that might have been among his best, else he would surely have led all the left-handers in history in every department. As it is he won more games (363) than any left-handed pitcher had ever won before. Also like Williams, Spahn played his first major league games in Boston. He joined the Braves in 1942 and in 1948 he helped the Braves to their first pennant in 34 years. In all his years with the Braves (23 including his 3 service years) Spahn had only two losing seasons. He won 20 or more games in 13 seasons. After the Braves let him go—with Spahn angrily protesting that he could still win—Warren joined the Mets where he struggled for part of the 1965 season to help that hapless club out of the cellar. He ended his big league career that year with the San Francisco Giants, where he won 3 games and lost 4. No other major league club would have him so Spahn, positive at the age of 44 that he could still win ball-games, joined the Mexico City Tigers as pitching instructor, with the understanding that he would have a chance to work on the mound. He pitched 10 innings in 3 games and won 1. He then signed as manager of the minor league Tulsa Oilers and pitched 7 innings (losing 1 game) there, before retiring to the coaching box. In 1971 he became pitching coach for the Cleveland Indians.

A wiry, grim-looking man, who seemed almost too frail to scare a batter, Spahn pitched with spectacular control, winding his curve and his get-em-out screwball endlessly around the batter's knees. He had one of the highest kicks in baseball, lifting his front foot so far above his head before he let the ball go, that the batter completely lost sight of the ball.

## CHARLES DILLON "CASEY" STENGEL, who set
records as a major-league manager surpassing those of

Warren Spahn of the
Milwaukee Braves
in the 1957
World Series.

Casey Stengel is wearing the insignia
of all the major-league clubs he was
associated with. There would not be room
to include all the minor-league clubs.

John McGraw and Connie Mack, still won his widest fame as the manager (after he had been retired for old age) of the most hapless club in baseball, the last-place New York Mets. His fame, which had been won when he managed the Yankees for 12 years and led them to 10 pennants and 7 World Championships, multiplied many times when he began to lead his beloved (but benighted) Mets around the circuit. Everywhere the club went its first season, Casey was greeted as a celebrity to be photographed, interviewed, cheered, and feted. His convoluted way of talking (always more involved in public discourse than in private) became known as "Stengelese" and he was quoted more frequently in the press than many a President.

But Casey, despite his latter-day public personality, and despite his frequent cutting-up during his playing days, was far from a professional clown. He was a shrewd, profoundly informed, aggressive, sharp-tongued, sharp-eyed, and calculating manager.

Casey set out to be a dentist, but gave up when he found the profession was not adjusted to left-handers. As a player, he was a better-than-average outfielder with many different minor- or major-league clubs. Undoubtedly his long and varied schooling in the game, and the knowledge he gathered of its thousands of tactical possibilities, all treasured in his fiercely retentive memory, helped make him a successful manager.

Casey's entry into organized baseball was inauspicious, for the first club he joined, at Kankakee, Illinois, lasted only halfway through the first season (1910) when the league disbanded. Casey finished the season with the Maysville club in another league, and hit only .223. In 1911, however, he led the Wisconsin-Illinois league with a batting average of .352. Nicknamed Dutch as a boy, he was known as Casey (after K.C., the city where he was born), by the time he graduated to the Brooklyn Dodgers in 1912. After 6 lively seasons in Brooklyn, where he left a trail of legends about his antics, he played 2 seasons in Pittsburgh and in 1919 was traded to the Phillies. Rather than play for cut wages, he stayed out of baseball the rest of the 1919 season and came to the Phillies in 1920.

In 1921, the Phillies sent him on to the New York Giants, where he played part-time and hit hard, posting averages both of his years in New York of over .300. He ended his career as a major-league player with the Boston Braves, who promoted him in May 1925 to the presidency and managership of their farm club in Worcester. It was here that he formed his close friendship with George Weiss, future general manager of the Yankees and president-to-be of the Mets. Weiss then operated the New Haven club in the Eastern League.

Casey fired himself as manager of Worcester, resigned as president, and accepted a job as manager of the Toledo Mudhens in the American Association. He held this job 6 seasons, winning the pennant in his second year and finishing in last place in his final year. He still played part-time while with Worcester and Toledo, stayed on the bench in Toledo in 1930, then came back in 1931 to wind up his playing career with 3 hits in 8 times at bat.

In 1932, he joined the Brooklyn Dodgers as a coach and became manager in 1934. His contract ran through 1937, but the owners let him go in 1936 and he liked to brag of being paid not to manage in 1937. When he lost his Brooklyn job, he was given a testimonial dinner by the New York sports writers.

In 1938, Stengel became manager of the Boston Braves, a collection of aging or semi-talented ball players not unlike the Mets, except that the Braves never quite made it to last place. After Casey had hoisted them to sixth place in 1943, he was fired and became manager of the Milwaukee club, whose absentee owner, Bill Veeck, away at war, tried hard to have him fired at once. But Casey worked out his contract and won the pennant. Then he joined the Yankee chain, first in Kansas City, then in Oakland, where he made a sensational first-place finish, with 114 victories in 1948. Weiss, who had become general manager of the Yankees, then brought his old friend to New York and they made a dazzling record together.

They left the Yankees at the same time and when Weiss joined the Mets he soon persuaded Stengel to join him there to help build the "image" and to deal with the temperamental and superannuated stars who dressed up the roster. But Casey proved best at teaching the game to the many green youngsters in the Met organization and he reveled in the newfound limelight. So explosive did his fame become that baseball's high brass arranged a special dispensation to allow him, on retirement, to enter the Hall of Fame without the usual waiting period.

## LLOYD JAMES WANER, who became known as

"Little Poison," was signed by the Pittsburgh Pirates in 1927 on the recommendation of his big brother, Paul "Big Poison" Waner. Lloyd promptly lived up to his brother's good word by leading the league in runs scored. Actually, Lloyd was a bit taller than Paul, although they weighed just about the same. Lloyd was a righty and Paul was a lefty, but they both hit from the left-hand side of the plate. They hit very much alike, too. In 1927, when Paul led the league with a .380 batting average, Lloyd was not far behind with .355. In the World Series, Lloyd batted .400 and brother Paul, .333.

In his first year in the majors, Lloyd set a mark for rookies with 223 hits. His 198 singles that year was just 1 short of the record. In 1929, he hit more triples than anybody else in the league, and in 1931, he got the most hits. Like his older brother, he was out to win ball games rather than set records. The high marks were just incidental to his trying every way he could to beat the enemy. Lloyd, like Paul, could run, throw, go back or come in after fly balls, steal bases, bunt, or hit behind the runner.

When Lloyd first came to the Pirates, he had not quite got his growth. He was five feet, seven inches, and weighed 145 pounds. He had been turned down by the San Francisco Seals and had played just one season in organized ball, with Columbia, South Carolina. Some of his elders predicted that he was too frail even to get through spring training. But he hit everything in sight that spring and, when the season opened, he started in left field. His first time at bat, with a man on base ahead of him, Lloyd beat out a drag bunt. Then brother Paul drove both runners in. From then on, there were two Waners in the lineup every day. And every day, almost, one or the other would be on base.

Both Waners hit with consistency. Lloyd, in his first 12 seasons, only twice dropped below .300. Lloyd was no long-distance hitter. He got extra bases on his speed. And, in his day, there was no one faster at going down to first base.

In temperament, the Waners were not at all alike. Paul was as merry as his middle name (Glee), liked to stay out late, and enjoyed making noise. Lloyd was quiet, given to regular hours, and went early to bed. He and Paul roomed together during most of their careers with Pittsburgh, but eventually Lloyd asked for a different roommate. He did not like being awakened after midnight by big brother, rolling home.

Both men had exceptionally bright eyes, that seemed to denote sharp vision. But Paul eventually wore glasses at the plate—and continued to hit. While both batted from the same side of the plate, they had different styles. Paul was the harder hitter and often drove balls on a line to right. But Lloyd's long hits, when he got them, were sliced to left field. Both men were skillful bunters. Lloyd, the most adept at getting on base, was the lead-off man. Paul, the solid hitter, batted third. And often both wound up on base together.

The Waners are the only brothers in the Hall of Fame.

**MICKEY WELCH,** like George M. Cohan and Calvin Coolidge, was born on the Fourth of July. A medium-sized, sturdy and imperturbable young man, he was one of the most durable athletes who ever lived. Mickey opened his big-league career in 1880 in Troy, N. Y. when that city was represented in the National League. He moved to New York

In Pittsburgh there was almost always a Waner on base. It was often Lloyd, known as "Little Poison".

Mickey Welch, one of the most durable athletes who ever lived, was a 300-game winner.

along with other stalwarts on the nine when, John Day, owner of the original New York Mets, bought the franchise of the dying Troy club and planted it in New York. (In the very same park as his Mets, who belonged to the American Association.)

Mickey went on to become the most reliable pitcher in the club, working in seventy or more games every season, and sometimes winning more than half of them. (In 1885 he won forty-seven games, seventeen of them in a row.) Hard work, bad decisions, errors by his teammates, lucky hits—none of these ever upset young Michael, who earned his nickname "Smiling Mickey" because of his indomitable good nature.

It was in 1885 that the New York club, named the Maroons but always called simply "the New Yorks," became the Giants when manager Jim Mutrie, in an excess of fervor, leaped to his feet at a victory and shouted "My big fellows! My Giants!" But Mickey, at 5 foot 9, was no giant, except in courage.

On August 28, 1884, Mickey Welch, pitching against Cleveland at the "old" Polo Grounds (which held two full baseball fields) struck out the first time nine men who faced him. He won the game 10 to 2. He finished that season with thirty-eight wins and twenty-two losses.

Mickey's big-league career, compared to that of some other greats, was relatively short—thirteen seasons altogether. But in that time he won 309 games. He was the last of the 300-game winners to be elected to the Hall of Fame.

# GEORGE MARTIN WEISS, of New Haven, Baltimore,
Newark, and New York, probably made a larger contribution to the game with less fanfare than did any other man in the whole history of baseball. A truly shy man who loved his work so dearly that he thought nothing of putting in eighteen hours a day on it, George, once he had reached the executive level of the game, always worked quietly behind the scenes. Indeed, some sports writers who covered the New

York World Series games did not recognize Weiss when he appeared in the locker room. Yet he was the man who had put together one championship team after another.

George Weiss began his baseball career when he was still in high school, acting first as manager of the school baseball club at New Haven High, then as manager of the New Haven Colonials, an amateur outfit made up mostly of the high-school team. The Colonials became semipros and George had them playing big-league clubs he imported to New Haven. Eventually, after winning the city championship and scoring many a triumph at the gate with his Colonials, Weiss became the owner of the local minor-league club and fashioned them into champions of the Eastern League. His greatest day in New Haven came when his New Haven club beat the great Baltimore Orioles, pennant winners of the International League.

Soon afterward, Weiss found himself running the Orioles, who had tumbled into the cellar. By shrewd trading and recruiting, George turned them into champions again and had the club making a profit at the gate. He was quickly signed by Colonel Jacob Ruppert to come build a farm system for the Yankees. Starting in Newark, where he won still more championships, Weiss built pennant winners for the Yankees in several minor-league cities, then moved at last to the big club.

As assistant to Edward Barrow and finally, as General Manager, George had full charge of the Yankee personnel for 15 years. There were, he said, always three Yankee teams in his mind—the club on the field, the one on the bench, and the club not yet put together from the minor-league players. As old stars diminished, Weiss invariably had new ones ready to move in, for he always planned several seasons ahead. At the same time, he knew that winning had to be done **this year,** so he made a speciality each season of bringing in a veteran or two, through trade or purchase, who could supply just the punch or the pitching needed to win that year's flag.

His proudest moment with the Yankees, he felt, came with the signing of Joe DiMaggio from the Pacific Coast League, a supposedly "damaged" player, but one whom George knew to be sound. He was able to secure DiMaggio because he had minor-league players—always more valuable than cash—to offer in exchange.

After winning 11 pennants with the Yankees, Weiss was involuntarily retired because of "old age." He moved then to the New York Mets and, before he retired for good, he had made them into champions. Thus he left baseball with an unblemished record of building a pennant winner with every club he operated.

**THEODORE SAMUEL WILLIAMS** was unique. No man ever lived who saw all of baseball's great hitters at their best. But some who saw most of them will agree with Ted's admirers that there was never a greater hitter than Ted Williams—not Ruth or Cobb or Wagner or Anson or DiMaggio or Heillman or Hornsby. The record book does not credit Williams with feats as great as some of those, but the record book fails to record that the years Ted Williams put in as a pilot in the service of his country through two wars were the years that ordinarily should have been his most productive.

Even so, Ted Williams is the last of the "modern" .400 hitters (he hit .406 in 1941), and he also led the American League four times in batting and four times in total home runs. His secret was a combination of exceptionally sharp eyesight (he is a dead shot with a rifle) and exceptionally close application. Perhaps no one other than Ty Cobb ever studied the business of batting more devotedly than Ted Williams did or practiced it more assiduously. From childhood, he immersed himself in baseball, playing it often from dawn to dusk and sometimes skipping meals to stay on the ball diamond. Like many great baseball players, Ted was originally a pitcher and he always owned an exceptionally strong throwing arm. With the Boston Red Sox, the only big-league club he ever played for, Ted actually pitched two innings (to no decision) in 1940, his second season in the majors.

But Ted was purchased by the Red Sox for his hitting and he showed the fans in Boston (some of whom used to berate him for what they thought was his lackadaisical playing) hitting power such as they had never seen, not even in the days of Babe Ruth and Jimmy Foxx. In 1946, when Ted led the Red Sox to a pennant, the opposition used to set up a special defense against him, known as the "Williams shift," that put the shortstop, the second baseman, and the first baseman all on the right side of the diamond, where they were supposed to nail any line drive off Williams's bat. This shift, which conceded Ted a single if he wanted to poke the ball to left, did choke off a few extra base hits that Ted might have got. But he scorned to give in to it and continued to hit to his power, often enough putting the ball far, far into the right-field stands, or over them, and piling up a solid batting average nonetheless.

To hear his critics, who found fault with his occasional absent-mindedness in the outfield, one might imagine that Ted was not earning his pay. But he could, and often did, throw runners out from distant spots in the grass and in 1951 he led all the American League outfielders in double plays.

A lively, ebullient, and friendly boy when he first broke into baseball, at the age of 17, with the San Diego club of the Pacific Coast League, Ted grew an inch or two and added many pounds to his skinny frame as he made his way upward in organized ball Knows as "The Splinter" with the Red Sox, he fleshed out to about 200 pounds before he retired. Along the way, his mercurial nature earned him as many devoted friends as it did earnest enemies. His uninhibited ways on the bench and on the basepaths, his clowning, and his breath-taking way of speaking his mind when he was a youngster in the minors occasionally drove his managers to despair. In the big leagues he often let his anger flare in public, dropped his clowning toward the fans, and was often the center of controversy. But his genius with

George Weiss's consuming passion was winning ball games. He wanted to win every day, and every season.

Ted Williams wrote a book about hitting, a subject he knew more about than any other man alive.

297

the bat (and with the glove, too) earned him the forgiveness and eventually the adoration of the fans. His openhandedness and the basic gentility of his nature won him a high spot in the hearts of many who knew him best, and even those who had felt (and resented) the rough side of his tongue knew he had earned a spot in baseball's Hall of Fame by a margin wider than many others'.

Because he took good care of his body (except in the heat of play), he lasted many more years in baseball than even he had expected he might. He performed astounding feats at the plate in many an All-Star game (he played in 18) and played out his string in the 1950 All-Star game after fracturing an elbow while making a spectacular catch against the wall. In the 1946 All-Star game, he made 4 hits and 4 runs in 4 times at bat; and he won the 1941 All-Star game with a home run. He also made a home run in his very last game in the big leagues, Sepember 28, 1960. It was number 521.

# EARLY WYNN, as a youngster, looked more like the

class grind than a baseball player. A solemn, determined-looking young man, he was reputed to be one of the toughest competitors who ever pitched in the majors. Some men used to say that Wynn would "knock down his mother" if she ever faced him with a bat in her hand. It is doubtful that Early would have gone that far. But once, when he was pitching batting practice before a game, he did knock down his own son with a tight pitch. The boy had begun to "lean in" a little on his dad's pitches and Early wanted to remind him that such liberties were not allowed.

Early, with 1 season and a bit more taken out for service in the armed forces, pitched 23 seasons in the majors, working his way, through sweat, courage, and determination, from low man on the staff to top pitcher in the league.

Wynn started in professional ball at age 18 with Sanford of the Florida State League, where he won 16 games his first year and was signed by the Washington Senators. After 2 years on the farm club in Charlotte, Early moved to the big club in 1939, lost 2 of the 3 games he worked, and went back to Charlotte. In 1941, he graduated to Springfield, in the Triple A Eastern League, where he won 16 games. He finished the season in Washington and stayed in the majors until 1963. Early won 18 games for Washington in 1943, but he put in his best years with Cleveland, where he was the workhorse of the staff throughout the 1950s. He won 20 games or better for Cleveland in 4 separate seasons, was traded to the White Sox in 1958, and won 22 games for them in 1959, leading his new club to the pennant.

Early was 43 years old when he won victory 300, to join the few pitchers in history who have touched that mark; to hear his contemporaries tell it, he never had anything but a whistling fast ball and a lot of determination. He seemed to hate the very sight of an enemy batter and would never allow the best of them to crowd the plate. He was, said Ted Williams, "the toughest pitcher I ever faced." His Indian forebears may have given the grim cast to his countenance that made him look so fearsome on the mound. But actually Wynn was a mild-mannered and soft-spoken man off the diamond and no man to vaunt himself unduly or attract attention to himself by flamboyant behavior. He just wanted to be recognized as boss when he was on the pitching mound.

## ROSS YOUNG first entered professional baseball with the Sherman, Texas, club of the Western Association. He had to keep telling writers, fans, and even coaches and managers that there was a "y" in his first name and an "s" on the end of his last name. By the time he reached the New York Giants, in 1917, when he was 19 years old, he had just about given up the struggle for Royce Youngs and allowed himself to be called Ross Young. This was the name he was known by through most of his major-league career, all of which he spent with the Giants.

A track and football star in school (West Texas Military Academy), Ross was determined to make good in baseball, despite football-scholarship offers from a dozen colleges. He tried out at second base with the Austin club of the Texas League when he was only 16, but could not find himself a job until he had landed with Sherman, farther down the ladder. On that rung, he hit .362 and the Giants signed him on.

Ross, who weighed 150 pounds when he first came to the Giants, never grew much larger. But he appealed to McGraw because he was full of fight. Trying out at third base, a job he just was not fitted for, Ross fought and scrambled and yelled. But he could not adjust to the infield. His arm was strong, but his aim was erratic. He was always in too much of a hurry to get the ball away, and his feet were always getting to the ball before his hands. But Ross could hit hard. He could run like a fox. And he could throw the ball in from deepest outfield.

So McGraw sent him to the minors for a while and told them to keep him in the outfield. When Ross came back to New York, in 1918, he became a regular. He hit over .300 every season, right from the start, except for the season of 1925. And he was consistently among the leaders in throwing runners out from right field.

Ross seemed at his best when the stakes were high. In the World Series, he could almost always be counted on to hit the ball hard and far. In the 1921 series against the Yankees, the first Ross played in, he drove out a triple and a double, knocked in 3 runs and scored 3. Next year, facing the Yankees again, Ross made 6 hits for an average of .375. In 1923, once more against the Yankees, he made 8 hits for an average of .348.

Ross, always a favorite of McGraw's, might have gone on to place himself among the leaders in every offensive department, for his speed made him a constant threat to score. But in 1925 he contracted Bright's disease, and all of the following season he needed a male nurse at his side to call a halt when Young seemed to be tiring. Ross died in 1927, only 30 years old, an age when many outfielders are just reaching the height of their skills.

Early Wynn made a habit of driving batters away from the plate with tight pitches.

A group of youngsters from Puerto Rico flock to Pirates star Roberto Clemente at Three Rivers Stadium.

**ROBERTO CLEMENTE** is one of organized baseball's true heroes. Unlike too many of the men who performed miraculous feats on the diamond, Clemente devoted much of his time, energy, and income to improving the lot of his poorer friends and neighbors. A man of active and wide-ranging intellect, Clemente involved himself in all sorts of causes far removed from professional athletics. And he died in the very act of trying to insure that relief supplies and moneys, collected to relieve the survivors of a devastating earthquake in Nicaragua, should reach those who needed them.

As a baseball player Clemente may have been the best who ever took money for playing. Certainly none of his contemporaries could outdo him in any aspect of play. He was a timely and consistent hitter, an aggressive baserunner, an outfielder who could make putouts in every corner of the field (he once actually threw a man out on a bunt), and the owner of perhaps the mightiest throwing arm in the game. Enemy baserunners often held their ground on "scoring" flies just out of respect for Roberto's strong and accurate arm. He was once said to have thrown a strike to home plate from 460 feet away.

Had Clemente played in New York, he undoubtedly would have earned wider fame, for he was as accomplished as any of the great Yankee heroes who became the big names in baseball. He did not break home-run records or drive balls so far that surveyors had to come to measure the distance. But Clemente played in Forbes Field in Pittsburgh, where it was nearly impossible to hit a fair ball out of the playing field. So he concentrated on line drives, and on timely blows designed to bring runners in to score.

True to his basic nature, Clemente was always a team player. He did not nurse his batting average by disdaining all pitches that missed the strike zone. One of his "faults" was his habit of reaching out for bad pitches when he had teammates in scoring position. But bad pitch or not,

Clemente could drive the ball into fair ground often enough to keep his batting average consistently above .300. And he is one of the eleven ballplayers of all time who collected more than 3,000 base hits.

Clemente was an earnest worker for bettering the lot of the average ballplayer, particularly the Latins. Although his own salary (said to be about $150,000 a year) was one of the highest in the game, he still stood ready to join the struggle to force the minimum salary higher. But he was no man to belittle his own ability. When he was asked how he rated himself as a player, he replied simply that he did not know anyone who could bat, throw, run, or field any **better** than he could. Nor could his questioner name anyone who could.

Clemente was often criticized for missing games because of injuries, which some writers suggested were imaginary. But Clemente suffered from many very real ailments and played often in spite of them. He had suffered with malaria, had severely injured both shoulders, had a damaged foot, a chipped elbow, and a spinal ailment that required the draining of fluid from his spinal column. He had broken several bones in the course of his career. Typical of Clemente was his response one day, after he had complained of severe soreness in his foot and had then gone flying from first base to score on a single. "I was in a hurry to get to the bench and rest my foot," said Roberto. Pain or not, Clemente never loafed. He used to charge top speed for first base on even the most "obvious" out. And he turned some outs into safe hits that way.

Clemente's lifetime batting average was .318 and he won the National League batting title four times. In 1966 he was named Most Valuable Player and in 1971 was named Outstanding Player in the World Series when he batted .414.

The Hall of Fame waived its five-year waiting period in order to honor this great man. But actually Roberto Clemente honors the Hall of Fame by his presence there.

## PHOTO CREDITS